Spiritual Healing with Children with Special Needs

Bob Woodward

Foreword by Hugh Gayer

Jessica Kingsley Publishers
London and Philadelphia

First published in 2007
by Jessica Kingsley Publishers
116 Pentonville Road
London N1 9JB, UK
and
400 Market Street, Suite 400
Philadelphia, PA 19106, USA

www.jkp.com

Library of Congress Cataloging in Publication Data

Woodward, Bob, M.Ed.
Spiritual healing with children with special needs / Bob Woodward.
p. cm.
Includes bibliographical references and index.
ISBN 978-1-84310-545-9 (pb : alk. paper) 1. Spiritual healing for children. 2. Children with disabili-
ties--Rehabilitation. 3. Teenagers with disabilities--Rehabilitation. I. Title.
RJ505.S658W66 2007
618.92'891656--dc22

2006100143

British Library Cataloguing in Publication Data
A CIP catalogue record for this book is available from the British Library

ISBN 978 1 84310 545 9

Printed and bound in Great Britain by
Athenaeum Press, Gateshead, Tyne and Wear

Dedicated, with gratitude, to all the children and their parents who have supported my spiritual healing work over the past four years.

Acknowledgments

I am grateful to the following people who gave their valuable time to read the draft copies of this book and then gave me the benefit of their qualified views and helpful suggestions: Dr Hugh Gayer, the Sheiling School's Medical Adviser; Etta Bateson, an experienced curative educator who very actively supported my spiritual healing sessions with children over the past year; Hazel Townsley who made legible, again, my handwritten manuscript.

Thanks to all my other colleagues at the Sheiling School in Thornbury, past and present, who gave their blessing to my spiritual healing practice with pupils, and also to my two first healing mentors, Dennis and Doreen Fare, without whose confidence in my abilities to become a healer none of this work would ever have been possible.

I am greatly indebted to all the parents and guardians who so readily gave their written consent for me to refer to their children's special needs and to my individual healing sessions with them.

My thanks also go to the editorial team at Jessica Kingsley Publishers.

Naturally I take sole responsibility for the contents of this book and also for any errors I may have, unwittingly, committed.

Contents

Foreword

In this unique book Bob Woodward has written of his spiritual healing work with the children and youngsters of the Sheiling School, where he lives. Those familiar with the children with special needs catered for in the various Camphill Schools will appreciate that it takes some skill and bearing to bring many of these children to stillness. They may be restless, hypersensitive, inwardly distressed, aside from their learning disabilities and, often, specific behaviour disturbances.

The Camphill curative educational approach epitomises a seamless integrated method, embracing residential houses, schooling, and therapeutic and medicinal input, within a rich Christian-based cultural life. Each child has an individualised programme into which all these areas carry their influence. How, then, can we assess the benefit of a specific activity such as spiritual healing in such a context?

The current method favoured for assessing the efficacy of medical treatments, 'evidence-based medicine', attempts to isolate one factor or treatment to produce a comparison of statistical probabilities of benefit. Among other concerns regarding this method, it cannot predict what will happen with any one patient!

An alternative method, 'cognition-based medicine' (best used in conjunction with what is useful from evidence-based medicine), is to start from, and consider, the whole context of the individual patient. Clearly, this lends itself better to complex, individualised approaches, such as with a child in a Camphill School. What has been ably described in this book is in keeping with this much more holistic and context-based approach. Furthermore, although Bob's healing work with children and youngsters has taken place within the specific Camphill setting, there may well be potential benefits for many more children in receiving spiritual healing sessions with suitably skilled practitioners. This much wider application of healing is clearly also Bob's hope.

The author has been modest in drawing conclusions from his observations. The genius of what can happen lies with the individuality of each child, and the unselfish love and care we can manifest. For those who have not read Bob's earlier book, *Spirit Healing* (Woodward 2004), I thoroughly recommend it for an understanding of what lies behind his healing work as presented in this new and timely volume.

Dr Hugh Gayer
The Sheiling School Medical Adviser

Introduction

My purpose in writing this book is to share my observations and experiences of giving spiritual healing, through the laying-on of hands, to some children and young people who have special educational needs. I hope that in doing so the possible benefits of offering spiritual healing to such 'special children' may be further, and sensitively, explored by those who are concerned with helping to alleviate their various disabilities and to reduce their inner frustrations, fears, and anxieties. I am not aware of any other publication which has specifically described giving spiritual healing to children and young people with special needs.

From a certain point of view I see this book as a complement and sequel to my previous volume, *Spirit Healing*, published in 2004, in which I attempted to examine spiritual healing from an anthroposophical perspective, and also included numerous practical examples of giving healing, mainly to adults. I did not, however, refer in *Spirit Healing* to my ongoing practice in offering healing to children with special needs, as I felt that this would go beyond the remit of what I wished to address at that time. That remit was essentially to ask, and to try to answer, the questions: 'Does spiritual healing work?' and 'How can we understand this form of healing?' It is of course one thing to give spiritual healing to adults who ask for this, and who are also then able to tell the healer what they experience and, in particular, if they feel they have derived some benefit and help from it, and it is quite another thing to give healing to children and young people with special needs who are usually not able to verbally articulate their experiences. Instead of such direct verbal feedback, careful observation of how an individual child is responding to receiving healing is called for as well as a very sensitive feeling and respect for the real, spiritual, being of the child. Fortunately I had more than 30 years experience in living with and educating such exceptional children before I began to have healing sessions with some of them, in response to the written request and consent of their parents or legal guardians. The dual combination of my being an experienced curative educator and also a qualified spiritual healer, is perhaps rather unusual, if not unique.

In this regard I am not aware of any other curative educator who is also a spiritual healer, nor do I know of other spiritual healers whose practice is primarily in giving healing to children with special needs. I therefore feel myself to be in a rather privileged position and, because of this, also to bear a responsibility to share some of my experiences gained thus far with a wider public than only my immediate colleagues.

However, I must point out that what is contained in this book with reference to my own healing practice, whilst certainly based on careful observation, is not in any sense a rigorous research investigation of the effects of giving spiritual healing to children with special needs. I am at present engaged in a modest part-time PhD research study along these more rigorous lines, within the Faculty of Health and Social Care at the University of the West of England; however, this research project will not be completed for another two years at the earliest. No, the healing practice described in this book is experiential and empirical and also anecdotal, and is based on my extensive written records of giving nearly 1000 individual healing sessions to pupils over a period of four years, from May 2002 to May 2006.

I am extremely grateful to the parents of these pupils for giving me permission to refer to my healing sessions with their children, though fic-titious names are used throughout to respect confidentiality. When I wrote to parents to ask if they were willing to give their consent for me to refer to my experiences and observations with their sons or daughters in such a book, I added that I felt that this form of healing 'may, possibly, be of benefit to many other children with special needs'. I did not, however, give any specific timing as to when I might begin to put pen to paper, let alone when the book might eventually be published. I was therefore both surprised and greatly encouraged when, already in December 2005, one of the parents wrote back to me, 'Dear Bob, best of luck with the book and could you let us know when it's completed as we'd like to have a copy'.

Knowing that I already have two readers now gives me the impetus to write this book during these Easter holidays, and to share my experiences without any further delay. I hope that the book will prove accessible and of interest to as wide an audience as possible, including fellow healers and curative educators, parents and teachers, and indeed everyone who is concerned about the welfare and progress of children who have special needs and learning difficulties.

Bob Woodward

CHAPTER 1

Spiritual Healing

At the outset it is necessary to give the reader a clear description of what spiritual healing is.

In the *Code of Conduct* of the National Federation of Spiritual Healers, dated January 2006, we find the following helpful definitions: 'Spiritual healing is restoring the balance of body, mind, and spirit of the recipient. It is a natural, non-invasive, holistic approach that has the intention of promoting self-healing, to bring a sense of well-being and peace to the recipient' (p.2). When referring to 'contact healing', as contrasted with the method of 'distant' or 'absent healing' when the recipient is not in the physical presence of the healer, we read in the *Code of Conduct* that:

> Contact healing is spiritual healing carried out in the presence of the recipient who may be seated or lying in a horizontal position. The healer may lay hands on the recipient or the hands may be held off the body (p.2)

Some experienced healers may perhaps object that if the healer's hands are not actually in direct physical contact, that is, touching the recipient's body, but are held 'off the body' that this is not strictly contact healing but rather a form of distant healing. However, such technicalities are not likely to be of first importance to any recipients of spiritual healing, whose priority will be to gain some tangible benefits from the healer's ministrations, and perhaps some urgent relief from actual bodily discomforts, for example, to treat a painful back condition. At any event the healer must describe to his or her patient what he intends to do before doing it, and this includes asking permission to touch the patient. If this is at all problematic then a hands-off method of giving the healing may be the only option. As will be seen later, in giving healing to children and young people with special needs, great sensitivity is required of the healer to sense and judge what degree of contact is acceptable, or not, to each individual recipient. Moreover, the healer will also need to be prepared to modify or adapt what may be his customary or standard procedure in giving healing according to the particular responses and reactions of the individual child.

The really essential and central concept with regard to spiritual healing is that it is described as being a safe and often effective means of helping to restore a person to a more balanced and harmonious state of body, mind and spirit. Indeed, to be in good health we need to achieve such a balance and harmony on all levels of our being, including the physical, emotional and mental levels. Sometimes it is perhaps even through the illness itself that a better state of balance and harmony can be achieved for the individual. This is not of course to suggest that we should do nothing to help the person towards a speedy and full recovery, but rather to recognise that illness often has something important to teach us and can even be essential for our personal development and inner growth.

There are nowadays many good and informative books available on spiritual healing (see Bibliography), and although there may well be minor variations in the way healing is described, explained and practised, the literature does provide us with a common ground of agreement about some essential points. One of these essentials is that the spiritual healer does not heal out of him or herself, but is rather the willing channel, or conduit, through which the healing energies can flow to the recipient, this of course being on the assumption that the patients are themselves open and willing to receive the healing flow. Healing cannot be imposed or forced on anyone against their will, and no genuine healer would ever attempt to do this.

Though it may not sound very flattering I have once been described, in my role as healer, as a 'hosepipe' or 'teapot'! In actual fact I am personally quite happy with these homely images because, in a very down-to-earth way, they do convey very well what I believe to be the spiritual healer's essential function. Therefore I have also often used these same descriptions when telling new patients what my task is as healer. It inevitably raises a smile, or laughter, which gets our relationship off to a good start!

Of course both a hosepipe and a teapot are simply the physical means by which water, or tea, are delivered where they are needed – be it the garden or the teacup – nothing more nor less. However neither of these channels or instruments would be of any practical usage if there was no water to pass through the hosepipe nor tea to be poured from the teapot. With this simple analogy in mind we can therefore ask the more profound questions, 'Where do the healing energies (the water or tea) come from?' and 'Who, or what, directs their flow?'

In the relevant literature we may read some diversity of views concerning these questions about the source, or sources, of the healing energies and how precisely they are being directed. Nonetheless the essential point in regard to spiritual healing is that there is common agreement that the energies, their quantities and qualities and direction, derive from a non-material, spiritual sphere of reality. The healer is purely the channel and not the source of healing.

The renowned English spiritual healer, Harry Edwards (1893–1976), found time to write a number of very insightful books based on his 40 or so years of practice. In what must, I think, be regarded as his most comprehensive work, entitled *A Guide to the Understanding and Practice of Spiritual Healing*, and published in 1974, he argues in his clear and consistent way the case for an intelligently directed administration of healing energies and forces, from a spirit realm. 'The intelligently directed healing forces emanate from a non-physical realm, but through healership such non-physical forces are transformed into physical effects' (p.74). A little later on he adds:

> What we can do, and this is of primary importance, is to train ourselves to attune to Spirit and so become more useful instruments for the spirit healing operators. The healing power comes through us and is not of us. (p.79)

For Edwards the notion of intelligent 'operators' or, to use the terms he most frequently employed, 'Spirit Doctors' or 'Healing Guides', was both a practical and existential reality. To a large extent this conscious and willing co-operation between those who are in spirit and healers working on the physical plane, continues to be a common ground of agreement for many experienced practitioners. Although 30 years have passed since

Harry Edwards, the great healer, made his own transition into spirit in 1976, the essentials of spiritual healing which he identified in his books still hold good today. The main difference between then and now is probably in the greater public and professional awareness of, and openness to, the positive contribution which healing has to offer in the field of healthcare. I know of at least one main London hospital where two healers are currently employed by the NHS (Buxton-King 2004).

Naturally there will also be many people, and even perhaps some of those who can testify to the efficacy of spiritual healing from their own experiences who, for whatever reason, find it difficult to accept the 'spiritual' aspects which I have briefly alluded to. They will, however, be very interested to hear about the possibilities of this form of healing to help overcome a wide range of ailments and to learn of its many good results. In a time when there is a widespread interest in alternative and complementary therapies and remedies, spiritual healing may be viewed in a similar light as Reiki, acupuncture, reflexology, homeopathy and so on. If it works for someone, all well and good. How it works and where it comes from may not be then the most pressing questions for people who, in the first place, simply need practical healing help. In regard to the real life subjects of this book, namely, children who have special needs of one sort or another, the uppermost question in their parents' minds will certainly be, 'Can spiritual healing in any way help my child?' I hope that in the main chapters of this book which deal with descriptions of practical hands-on healing sessions, and which really form 'the living heart' of the book, an answer to this urgent question may begin to emerge. Through examining many short case studies we will see if spiritual healing appears to have been beneficial in meeting the specific needs of individual children.

However, in order to set my own experiences and observations of giving healing into the actual context in which they have taken place, I must first briefly say something about 'curative education' with children with special needs and about Camphill as a special form of provision and environment for the education of such children. This will therefore be the tasks of the next two short chapters.

For those readers who do wish to enquire further and more deeply into the theory or theories underlying the practice of spiritual healing, I would suggest that the books listed in the Bibliography are a good place to start. Anyone interested in a specifically anthroposophical perspective on spiritual healing may find my own earlier book, *Spirit Healing*, enlightening – at least I hope so! Finally for people who want a much more scientific and rigorous approach to the subject, the various volumes in Dr Daniel J. Benor's *Healing Research* series can be recommended.

CHAPTER 2

Curative Education

This book is not about curative education *per se*. However, since in addition to being a qualified spiritual healer, I am, by training and profession, a curative educator experienced in teaching and living with children with special needs, I feel it is appropriate to describe certain essentials of the art of curative education and the 'philosophy' which underpins it, namely anthroposophy. In actual fact what may be justly referred to as 'curative' or 'healing' education has a history which goes back into the eighteenth and nineteenth centuries with such pioneers as Jean Itard (1775–1838), Edouard Séguin (1812–1880), and Heinrich Pestalozzi (1746–1827) (Luxford 1994). However, the curative education and the profession of being a curative educator which is the subject of this chapter, is specifically based on the holistic anthroposophy, or 'Spiritual Science', of Rudolf Steiner PhD, the Austrian philosopher, educator and scientist, who is perhaps best known as being the founder of the mainstream Steiner or Waldorf Schools. The original Waldorf School (so named after the Waldorf-Astoria cigarette factory) was opened in Stuttgart in 1919. Since that time the Steiner School Movement has become the largest independent school movement in the world. The Waldorf School Curriculum is very clearly child-centred and in a wonderful and organic way it both supports and harmonises the various stages and phases of normal child and adolescent development. According to Steiner's anthroposophy and as described by him in numerous educational lecture courses, including those which he gave to the original group of teachers at the Waldorf School in Stuttgart, the phases of development which a person normally goes through from birth until early adulthood are underpinned by the incarnation of the individual's soul and spirit into his or her physical, material body. This also gives rise to the various inner faculties such as fantasy, imagination and thinking, which unfold during this differentiated process of growing up. Prior to conception the individual is purely a being of soul and spirit and lives in the spiritual world. After birth, he or she begins, quite literally, the slow descent to earth and is destined, if all goes well, to become a fully-fledged and able citizen of this physical world. The foundation for this process of incarnation and all the subsequent steps and stages of development and maturation is laid, after the child's birth, in the first three years of life. It is in these crucial early years that the monumental human achievements of walking, talking and thinking, and also the acquisition of a germinal self-awareness, are normally made (see König 1969). However, in very many children who are diagnosed as having special educational needs, specific abnormalities of development are to be found sometime during these very important first three years of life and the consequences of these may well then impact on his or her entire lifespan. In other words the child grows up suffering from some form of 'developmental handicap' or 'disability'.

Curative or healing education then has the task of helping and supporting the child or young person to overcome his or her disability, as far as this is possible, during the formative years of childhood and adolescence. It is a task and an art which calls for particular qualities, abilities and skills, in those who aspire to become qualified and competent 'curative educators'.

The cornerstone or foundation of all anthroposophical curative education is to be found in the course of 12 lectures which Rudolf Steiner gave to a group of around 20 people; medical doctors and aspiring curative teachers, at Dornach in Switzerland in 1924. To this day the detailed insights and substance given in these lectures prove themselves, again and again, to be a living wellspring of inspiration, knowledge and understanding, for curative work with children who have special needs. As with the anthroposophical understanding of normal child development, it is likewise the recognition of the incarnation-process of a child's real being, of soul and spirit, into a physical and material earthly body, which underpins the art of curative education and the practice of curative educators. This recognition and appreciation of each child's real spiritual being, or ego, is very important when trying to understand the obstacles and organic impediments which stand in the way of achieving a normal integration and incarnation into the body, and also then to do everything possible (educationally, medically, therapeutically) to foster a more healthy and harmonious development for each individual. Herein lies a tremendous responsibility and challenge, which calls for much patience, perseverance, humility, understanding, compassion and love. It is definitely not a task for the timid or the faint-hearted!

In the Introduction to the 1998 edition of Steiner's Curative Education Course, Albrecht Strohschein, who was one of those young educators who attended the lectures, writes the following, recalling an earlier meeting with Rudolf Steiner:

> He spoke so impressively of how these 'abnormal' children cannot incarnate completely with their ego and astral body (i.e. spirit and soul), and for this reason are already concerned with shaping a future earthly life, that we could only listen and take it in with all our senses.

> The impression was so great that later none of us could give a connected account of all that he had said. I know that when at the end I asked what such a difficult earthly life really meant for the souls of the so-called pathological or feeble-minded children, Rudolf Steiner waited a little while and then quietly replied, 'When in my investigations I look back, starting from the genius of today, I always find that a genius has gone through at least one such feeble-minded incarnation'. (Steiner 1998, p.3–4)

Siegfried Pickert, another young curative teacher, remembered that Dr Steiner had said, 'When I visit the class for mentally handicapped children at the Stuttgart Waldorf School, I say to myself, "Here one is working for the next earth-life, quite apart from what is accomplished now, which however can be a very great deal"'(Steiner 1998, p.4).

In these remarks, as also in the lectures of the Curative Education Course, we see how concretely Steiner spoke of the child's incarnation from a realm of spirit into earthly life and of the realities of karma and reincarnation. Of course I appreciate that many of these concepts may seem novel and strange, if not decidedly 'way out', to the reader who encounters them for the first time and is unfamiliar with Steiner's teachings. Nonetheless, to meet a child who has severe learning difficulties and special needs, if one has lived with and taken seriously such existential anthroposophical concepts, leads both to a deepened therapeutic relationship and also to a deepened respect for the child's innermost being, as well as an empathy for the difficult destiny which has been taken on in this present lifetime for whatever reasons.

In the course of my 30 or so years living with and teaching children with special needs and learning disabilities, I have encountered a wide variety of pathological constitutions and conditions including; autism; epilepsy; hysteria (i.e. emotionally over-sensitive children); cerebral palsy; post-encephalitis; aphasic and other communication disorders; and also different syndromes such as Down's, Lowe's, Coffin-Lowry, Cornelia de Lange, Fragile X, Asperger's, etc. However, whatever the condition or syndrome that a child has as its medical diagnosis, it is the meeting with the child's unique individuality and the creating of a mutual therapeutic relationship between child and educator which is of the first importance in the field of curative, healing, education. In this sense I have, for example, given clear emphasis to the need to establish a good therapeutic relationship with children on the Autistic Spectrum in the book *Autism – A Holistic Approach* (Woodward and Hogenboom 2002) in which detailed accounts of one-to-one therapeutic sessions and of individualised intervention exercises with two boys are described. In many respects it is actually the child with special needs who is the teacher and inspirer of the curative educator!

Anthroposophical curative education has by now been practised for more than 80 years. My own experience of this discipline and art has been entirely within the Camphill Community setting and since this is also the environment in which I have been able to practise spiritual healing, I will give a quick sketch of this particular context and environment in the next short chapter.

CHAPTER 3

Camphill Schools

The International Camphill Movement comprises village and urban communities, colleges of further education and training, and schools, for and with people who have special needs of one description or another. Since its modest beginnings in the north of Scotland, near Aberdeen, in 1940, Camphill has grown into an organisation that has around 100 centres distributed in 22 different countries around the world, from Norway to South Africa, from the USA to Russia (Pietzner 1990; Luxford and Luxford 2003). The majority of these Camphill places are communities of adults, whilst a minority (around 16) are schools. One of these is the Sheiling School Camphill Community in Thornbury, near Bristol, which was started in 1952, and where I have lived together with my family for nearly 30 years. There have been many changes over these years not least in the number of pupils, from around 80 in 1970, to currently around 20. This particular change is probably partly indicative of the wider development in increased and also integrated educational provisions for children with special needs in our society as a whole. Nonetheless there will no doubt always be a place for good residential special schools including Camphill centres, in order to meet the very pressing inclusive needs of some special children and their families.

Although a school, a better and truer term to describe where I live and work is, I think, a 'therapeutic community'. In common with other Camphill Schools, and as a therapeutic community, it has been based for many years on Steiner's anthroposophical understanding of the human being and has provided a holistic and wholesome environment for the practice of curative education. It is an environment in which many children have flourished over the past years.

This environment includes a lifestyle which is well structured and also rhythmical in its daily, weekly and annual patterns, and yet has room for spontaneity and creativity, for example, in classes and in recreational activities. The celebration of the main Christian festivals and also of lesser known festivals, such as Michaelmas in the autumn and St John's at mid-summer, gives the whole community of children and adults familiar and meaningful landmarks to prepare themselves for in the cyclical course of the year. Other communal events, such as termly school festivals, concerts, puppet plays and talks, also contribute to a rich and varied cultural life. The celebration of weekly non-denominational school services appropriate to the different ages of the pupils, provides special spaces to come to stillness and peace.

The curative organisation, or rather organism, of the therapeutic school community is essentially threefold, consisting of: school, home-life, and specific therapies and treatments. That is to say, the child with special needs lives in (or is 'attached' to in the case of day pupils), one of the residential houses on the school estate; goes from there to join his or her peers in the appropriate class in school; and when in school may be taken out of lessons in order to receive a specialised therapy, such as remedial eurythmy or, over the past four years at the Sheiling School, spiritual healing. Tempting though it would be to describe here at some length the holistic therapeutic environment and the wide diversity of provisions in a Camphill School, this is not necessary for the main purpose of this book, which is to share my experiences of offering spiritual healing to such children. However for those who do wish to hear more of the many provisions available for children with special needs in a Camphill Community setting, I can thoroughly recommend two books; *Education for Special Needs: Principles and Practice in Camphill Schools* by Henning Hansmann (1992), and *Holistic Special Education: Camphill Principles and Practice*, edited by Robin Jackson (2006). They give comprehensive and inspiring pictures of the life and work in Camphill Schools and, in the latter book, the most current practice and university training for curative educators is included.

Returning now to the theme of spiritual healing, I have to point out very clearly that this is not a provision or 'therapy' which is at all usual or common to Camphill Schools. Indeed, to the best of my knowledge it is, so far, unique to the Sheiling School in Thornbury. It is therefore important to say precisely how this has come about before launching into the fascinating description of healing sessions with individual children in the chapters which follow.

I qualified as a full healing member of the 'Bristol District Association of Healers', and the 'World Federation of Healing' in the summer of 2001, after successfully completing the two years of training as a probationer. Being keen to offer the possible benefits of spiritual healing to our pupils and feeling, after careful consideration, that spiritual healing was not in any sense contrary to the essential impulses of anthroposophical curative education or Camphill, I then began to explore how this might be achieved with the support of the school community. The outcome of the very constructive discussions which then took place was the proposal by our Medical Adviser that the parents of our pupils be informed by letter that I was, in addition to being a very experienced curative educator, now also a fully qualified 'healer' and that I was willing to offer healing sessions to pupils at the school if parents asked for this on behalf of their son or daughter and also gave their written consent. In this way the onus would be on the parents to request healing sessions and I would then, time allowing, endeavour to meet their wishes. Therefore, whilst both the school and our Medical Adviser were fully supportive of this new initiative, my spiritual healing work would have a certain 'independence' from the anthroposophical therapeutic activities normally provided by the school. Moreover, it was pointed out to parents that healing would be given through direct hands-on contact and that it therefore depended on the willingness of their children to receive such tactile contact, as demonstrated by their behaviour in the actual sessions. No prior claims were made as regards any benefits from the one-to-one sessions, but certainly a positive influence was suggested by stating: 'While it remains to be seen in what ways healing may benefit any of our pupils, it has been the experience of adults that a healing session provides a restful and peaceful period of relaxation, and often also a sense of well-being' (from a letter sent to parents dated 27 March 2002).

It was quite unknown at that time how many, if any, parents might take up the offer for them to request healing for their children. However responses were not long in coming and in the first year, beginning in May 2002, I gave regular healing to 16 of our pupils.

A room for this was available in 'Chalice', our purpose-built therapy building, and as this space had been used some years before as a play therapy room, it was found to be very appropriate for this new activity in its décor, size and feel. As with other individualised therapies, children came to me for healing on a one-to-one basis from their school lessons. For the healing nothing more was expected of the children than that they would be willing to sit more or less still on a soft covered stool or a chair, and also be willing for me to lay my hands lightly on them. Generally in the first years another adult was not present during healing sessions with the children, but in certain cases this was a requirement. For example, one boy's parents were perfectly happy that he received healing provided that his housemother was also present; whilst with a non-speaking young girl I myself requested that she be accompanied by a familiar female co-worker in order to help her to settle into this therapeutic situation. However, in my fourth year of healing practice, an experienced colleague was always present in the sessions acting as a third-party observer for the purposes of my healing research work.

In giving contact healing it is customary for most healers to follow a structured and consistent pattern with regard to the manner of the laying-on of hands. Not that this is absolutely set in stone, so to speak, because there must always be room for adaptability depending on a patient's particular needs. In giving children healing I have come to follow the procedure as outlined below, once the child has entered the room and is sitting on the stool or a chair. For complete clarity it should be said that all healing sessions take place with the child fully dressed and there is of course no touching of any intimate body parts.

1. I stand behind the child and place my hands lightly on his/her shoulders. The purpose here is to make the initial physical contact with the child and also to attune myself to the healing intention by becoming still and peaceful within myself. I also ask inwardly for the healing help to be given, as needed for each particular child.

2. Then I move my hands to his or her head.

3. I move my hands to his or her spine; one hand near the top and the other hand near the base of the spine.

4. Then, sitting down to one side of the child, I place one hand on (or over in the case of females), the heart area and the other hand on the corresponding area of the back.

5. I place hands as above, but on the solar plexus region in front and back.

6. Then, kneeling down in front of the child I place my hands on his or her feet, and sometimes also on the knees.

7. I then stand once again behind the child and put my left hand on the top of his or her head and my right hand at the base of the spine; a placement I call 'top and tail'.

8. To finish, I stand behind the child and again place my hands on his or her shoulders. However, over the course of recent practice I have also become used to slowly moving both my hands at the end of the session from above the child's head in a downward curved movement, as it were through their surrounding energy field. I repeat this movement three times.

As already mentioned, depending on the specific needs and the willing-ness of each child to receive healing, there can be variations in this general procedure. For example, one boy whom I saw regularly had an abnormal accumulation of fluid in his left lower leg and therefore I often omitted some of the usual hand positions in order to spend more time working on his swollen leg. With another boy who showed himself to be very sensitive to any hand placement near, let alone touching, his head, I spent much more time over his heart area than I did with most other children.

Individual sessions, usually weekly, could last from 10 to 30 minutes, again dependent on the needs and co-operation of each child and I was, in the first years, in the habit of having some appropriate (i.e. relaxing and harmonious) taped music playing during the session. However, already in the third year of practice I dispensed with this background music and found that this then led to a deeper experience of inner peace and quiet in the sessions.

Having thus set the scene, so to speak, for my healing sessions within the wider therapeutic Camphill context in which I work, I now very much look forward to sharing with you my numerous experiences and observations with particular pupils. In order to give you, the reader, a real feel for the situation with each child, many examples of actual healing sessions taken from my notes and records made at the time are reproduced in the next three chapters. To some extent these notes are repetitive but I feel it is very important to try to have a sense of *the whole series* of sessions and the qualitative process undergone with each pupil. With each child this was indeed a unique and special journey.

The short case studies which will now be given can rightly be said to form 'the heart and soul' of this book. To write them up has provided me with the opportunity to turn once more to my extensive healing records from recent years, and to recall vividly to mind the exceptional pupils with whom I have been allowed to work and also from whom I have learnt a great deal. Without question each one is a special and unique personality in his or her own right and deserves to be fully appreciated as such.

For purposes of confidentiality all the names of the children are fictitious and I will only give minimal, but nonetheless accurate information regarding each child's particular special needs, learning difficulties and characteristics.

So, as one of my current pupils often positively remarks at the start of her healing sessions with me, 'Here we go then!'

CHAPTER 4

Healing Sessions I

Steven, diagnosed with Sturge Weber Syndrome and epilepsy

When I first took Steven for healing in May 2002 he had been a pupil at the school for nearly 12 years. Now he was 18 years old and in the seniors class. Steven had multiple disabilities, being diagnosed with Sturge Weber Syndrome; severe learning difficulties; epilepsy; a left-sided hemiparesis; and glaucoma. He was a generally friendly, well-built, sturdy young man with a strong personality. He could easily become rather excitable and loud, though not in our healing sessions. In addition to all his other disabilities, Steven had no useful speech but could only make noises. When younger he had been prone to frustration tempers. He had made good progress over his years at the school, and had had some individual speech and eurythmy therapies. However, during the period that he had spiritual healing, Steven was not having any other individualised therapies.

Session 1 — 13 May 2002

Steven came with me from the pottery. He sat still and quietly to receive healing. He's sensitive on his head, and therefore I kept my hands at a distance. Was OK for me to hold his hands, and to touch his arms and legs. He had no objection to this. He is hemiplegic with left side affected. Also epileptic and no speech. Steven was co-operative.

Session 2 — 16 May 2002

Steven sat peacefully for healing. He fiddles his less able left hand and fingers, with his right hand. However, he became still, and he let me take his hands. Very sensitive on his head, so I still work at a distance there. I felt warmth over his throat area – he has no speech.

When Steven came out of Chalice (the therapy building) after healing, and stepped out into the bright light he had a seizure. He simply remained standing – eyes up and away. I called him back. He recovered himself completely and walked with me to Cinnabar (the seniors building).

By the end of the fourth session, a week later, Steven now had no objection to me actually touching his head.

Session 5 – 27 May 2002

Steven came down to Chalice with a huff and a puff – quite excitable. He was over-breathing. I said he could calm down, there was no rush. In the session he was peaceful and calm. After the session he walked calmly back to Cinnabar with me, and not in the excitable state in which he had come.

There was then a week's half-term break when all the pupils at the school return to their homes. After this holiday Steven's housemother at the school told me that he appeared to have had a good half-term at home, and his parents had said there were no problems or seizures. We continued with our weekly healing sessions in all of which Steven could come to times of stillness and quietness, in spite of his characteristic rather excitable and restless nature.

The last healing session for the summer term, in July, was quite typical.

Session 10 – 8 July 2002

Steven was very excitable on the way down and also restless to begin with in the session. However, he settled down and was at times very still, quiet and peaceful. It is impressive to see Steven when he is really sitting still and at peace.

After the long summer holidays we resumed our sessions in early September in the new school year. His housemother told me that he had been very noisy to begin with in the new house setting. (He had had a change of houses.)

Session 12 – 9 September 2002

Steven has a restlessness about him. He plays with his weak left hand with his good right hand. He certainly isn't relaxed and at peace. However, in the healing he can become more still and quiet. His weak left hand was warmed through; it felt as warm as his right. (The experience of warmth is a very common one in giving spiritual healing.)

Steven is co-operative in the session.

To try to bring this restless fellow to more peacefulness and to balance his energy left/right to help overcome his left-sided hemiplegia – these would be my aims.

Session 15 – 30 September 2002

Steven was unusually still and peaceful in this session. No fiddling with his fingers at all. Really remarkably peaceful.

There was a fortnight's half-term break in October and then we resumed in November and into December.

Session 19 – 19 November 2002

Steven was again co-operative. Not especially restless with his hands, though he 'plays' with his left-hand fingers with his right. Peaceful and still.

Session 21 – 2 December 2002

Steven was fine today. When I placed his hands on his legs, to curtail him fiddling with his fingers, he kept them there for some time and he was more restful.

After the session I saw him using his weak left hand to also get his scarf and hat on, i.e. not just relying on his stronger right hand.

Steven's housemother reported to me that in the first half of the long autumn term – from September to mid-October – he had been 'well and happy' in the house and that he had become 'less noisy'. For the second half of the term, from early November to mid-December, she reported that Steven 'had been good' and, as there were no further changes reported in his behaviour, he had also continued to be 'less noisy' than he was at the start of the term.

We resumed our sessions in the New Year, in January 2003.

Session 23 – 20 January 2003

I took Steven for healing today. In Cinnabar I was quite impressed to see how he put on his anorak with some help.

He was calm, quiet and peaceful in the session. Fiddling a bit with his left hand but when I placed his hands on his legs to be still, he complied with this.

Session 30 – 24 March 2003

I took Steven as usual. He did not object that I touched his head. His hands were warm. He is still and peaceful in the session.

In this thirtieth session we had a visit from an outside professional, Jim, who sat in to observe. Steven was due to leave the school at the end of the spring term 2003 due to his age, and Jim was getting to know Steven in order to support his change to a new, adult, placement.

Our last session, Number 32, took place in April, and once again Steven was co-operative and very willing to receive hands-on healing, as he had been throughout the year.

Shortly after Steven left us a telephone call was received in the school office from our visitor, Jim. He had apparently been very impressed with seeing just how quiet and calm Steven had been in the healing session that he had observed, and he wanted to arrange that Steven would continue to have healing in his new placement. I was therefore asked to write a report for the 'new' healer, to describe exactly what I had been doing with Steven. I was of course happy to do this and ended my report by saying, 'It was rather impressive to see just how peaceful Steven was in these sessions, which lasted up to half-an-hour each'.

We shall see, again and again, in the journal notes of other children's healing sessions, how a special space was created in which stillness and peace, calmness and quiet, could replace restlessness and disquiet – perhaps, metaphorically, like an oasis in which to stop and renew one's energies on the demanding journey of life.

Jane, diagnosed with Dystrophic Syndrome with coronal synostasis and epilepsy

Jane was another strong personality, also aged around 18, and in the seniors class at the school. Considering her early history and development it was altogether a wonder that she had reached early adulthood! Diagnostically she was described as having Dystrophic Syndrome with coronal synostosis; epilepsy; hearing loss; scoliosis; severe learning disability; and behavioural and sleep problems.

The most obviously striking thing about Jane's appearance was how short and stocky, and stiff-looking, she was for her age. Behaviourally she was very attention-seeking and demanding, and both going off to sleep, and sleeping through the night, were still major problems. Unlike Steven she did have some speech and was able to communicate in short phrases.

However, Jane certainly had a mind of her own and was a force to be reckoned with! She could, both in the school and in the house, be sometimes very obstinate, controlling and uncooperative. It was precisely because of her great needs that, following the parents' request and consent, I agreed to take her for healing sessions.

Jane is a case in point where my long experience as a curative educator was very much needed, in addition to my role as a spiritual healer. It might be that even a very experienced healer who has not encountered children and young people with such complex needs could feel rather at a loss how to proceed. As will become clear in describing some of the sessions, I was determined to persevere and do whatever I could to help Jane in spite of, at times, rather difficult behaviours from her. However, these sorts of behaviours were certainly not peculiar to the healing sessions, but were well known across the board, so to speak. As I have previously said, no qualified healer, myself included, would ever wish to force healing on any person against their will. Indeed any such wish could only be counter-productive! Nonetheless, with many exceptional children it is essential that clear limits and expectations of behaviour are given, as much as for their own feelings of safety and security as for the appropriate management of any given situation. Those who have experience in this field will, I am sure, know exactly what I refer to and the genuine curative educational spirit in which it is meant.

Session 1 – 15 May 2003

So a bit of a struggle to get Jane down to Chalice. She put herself on the ground a couple of times. However, I made my intentions very clear and she co-operated then.

I kept this first session short, but still had to insist that it would finish when *I* said. It went OK, and there was no problem in going back with me to Cinnabar. Her teacher tells me that the main difficulty with Jane is her 'mood swings'.

Session 2 – 19 May 2003

Jane came willingly with me to Chalice when I met her and the other seniors coming with their teacher from Cinnabar.

In the session she was quiet and still, but then was also several times getting up off the stool. I made my expectations clear, verbally, and she sat again. However, Jane seemed to get frustrated and hit herself (as she does), hitting her own arm or leg hard. No attempt to hit me.

After the session she walked back, hand in hand with me, to join her teacher. I will have to see how things progress. Jane is very small, compact and stiff. Can she be helped to relax? Can one strengthen the middle/breathing/balancing realm? One can try!

Session 3 – 22 May 2003

Jane was reluctant to come down to Chalice but I made it clear she *was* coming, and she did.

In the healing she sat still on the stool and was relaxed – no hitting herself. She's sensitive around her head, but I could put my hands on her back and also over the upper chest and solar plexus areas. Jane co-operated. She asked about 'Mummy' and 'going home', and wanted me to say 'Yes, Jane'. So, a positive session.

Session 4 – 26 May 2003

It worked well today. She seemed more relaxed and sat still, and was receptive to what I did. I was able to put my hands in the main positions – head, spine, chest, solar plexus.

The one-week summer half-term came and went, and we continued, as in the following examples.

Session 7 – 25 June 2003

I fetched Jane from Cinnabar. She made a big fuss, putting herself on the ground etc. However, in the session, she was co-operative – though getting off the stool quite often. A couple of times she leant over to me. Jane didn't pull her hair or hit herself at all. However, it seems difficult for her just to relax.

Session 8 – 30 June 2003

Well, although a little reluctant to come with me from Cinnabar, there were no fusses on the way to Chalice today.

In the session Jane co-operated, though indicated that she wanted to go out as soon as possible! I work around her (at a distance), rather than being too direct. A positive session I would say.

She's stiff in her constitution – like wood. Needs help to soften up, to become more pliant and flexible.

Session 9 – 2 July 2003

Had a very good healing session with her today. She was *much more relaxed and amenable*, and made no attempt to get off the stool. No fusses coming down, nor returning.

It seemed that my, or our, perseverance was paying off and an observation which her teacher made around this time was, I felt, significant, namely that in movement lessons (eurythmy), Jane had been doing very well in *imitating* actions. This was something I also observed when, at the end of a healing session, she imitated the curved movements I made with my arms.

There were two further sessions before the summer term came to an end and then the long summer holidays ensued. When we started the new school year in September Jane's housemother reported to me that Jane had apparently been uncooperative at home in the holidays, and that sleeping was a problem.

Session 12 – 8 September 2003

Her teacher brought Jane to Chalice. When she came into the healing room she cried and fussed. However, this soon stopped. In the session she got up off the stool numerous times, but I pointed (literally just pointing at the stool) that she should sit down again, which she did. So in this 'up and down' way we carried on! Afterwards I walked her back to Cinnabar.

Jane is very compact, dense, with tight muscles. Her hands are rather stiff – certainly not limp! – her calf muscles are tense also. So she needs to learn to relax and release bodily tension. I'll see her twice weekly and hope, over time, that she relaxes more.

Session 14 – 25 September 2003

I fetched Jane from Cinnabar as she had not been brought down to me. She made some fusses on the way to Chalice.

The session itself was good. She remained sitting on the stool through-out! Allowed me to place my hands on her. The main aim is to get her to relax more – her body is very stiff and 'wooden'. Interestingly she was moving her foot in the session, swinging it round. This was better I thought than being too uptight.

After the session Jane was reluctant to go past her house and return to her teacher, but it was not difficult to insist that she did and to gain her com-pliance.

I try to take a firm but reassuring tone towards her. Back with her teacher she put herself onto the ground. He says that she's either very good or very bad at present. She swings between the two extremes.

Session 16 – 6 October 2003

Her teacher brought Jane down to Chalice. She sat on the stool – actually throughout the session. Near the start of the session Jane began to hit herself; aggression directed entirely at herself, not at me. There was no obvious cause or trigger for this behaviour. She slapped her head and also pulled her hair. After this she settled down and was *remarkably composed and calm*, and appeared quite happy – actually smiling. Her hands were also less stiff and more relaxed than is often the case with her. I was therefore very pleased with her response. We finished and she walked back with me.

We continued our healing sessions after the two weeks of autumn half-term.

Session 19 – 6 November 2003

I see Jane just once a week now. Her teacher brought her down.

Jane came into the room willingly enough and sat down on the stool. However, she didn't allow herself to relax in the session, at times striking her face or pulling her hair. (As she does elsewhere, not only in a healing session!) However, I took a firm line with her and expected her to behave herself. Afterwards she walked back with me, hand in hand, to the Weavery (weaving workshop) without any fuss.

I feel that I should persevere with Jane, on a weekly basis. Fortunately at times in the session she is 'more relaxed', less tense and is co-operative.

Basically she is unkind with herself and engages in self-harm and abuse. She never attempts to strike me. She is very tight in herself – squeezed in – and finds it difficult to 'let go' and be.

I did persevere and, in the New Year, many good and positive sessions with Jane took place, of which I can share a few typical examples with you.

Session 24 – 22 January 2004

We had the best session so far I would say! Jane was more relaxed, receptive and peaceful. She did not reject my hands touching her. She got off the stool two or three times briefly, but sat down when I indicated. Walked properly back with me to Cinnabar afterwards.

Session 25 – 29 January 2004

Another very positive session. She was quiet and peaceful throughout. Jane got up a couple of times but sat at once back on the stool. She was smiling and seemed unusually happy and content.

And later, after the short half-term break.

Session 28 – 4 March 2004

Jane was in a very amenable mood today. She sat still and allowed touching. Did not hit herself once. More contented and 'happy' than I've seen her before. She had already come to the session in a 'good' mood.

Her main carer also told me that Jane had been in a good mood this week, was sleeping well and was more relaxed.

Session 30 – 18 March 2004
Exceptionally still, peaceful and quiet today from the moment she sat on the stool. Receptive, and did not hit herself at all – nor has she done so for the last few sessions since half-term.

In the main Jane continued in this receptive and co-operative state in the sessions we had through to the end of June. In the thirty-fifth session *she* initiated putting her arms around me, which she had not done before, and in the last session of the year she was reluctant to leave the healing room, as described below.

Session 37 – 28 June 2004
Jane was in an unusually cheerful mood when she came in – laughing a little. She found it difficult to settle peacefully and stood up a number of times. However, she then settled down and was receptive.

   However, at the end she didn't want to go; nor did she want me to get up, but to sit down! Eventually I had to insist that she must go, and I also, and then she made a fuss! And she continued to make a protest on the way back towards Cinnabar, jumping off the ground and then putting herself down on the ground. I let her get up in her own time. She was focused on the prospect of soon going home.

My initial decision to offer Jane healing in spite of her sometimes difficult and challenging behaviours, was borne out of a recognition of her very particular special needs including, I believe, a deeply seated existential fear and anxiety.

   Overall I would say that Jane had made clear progress through the sessions over that year of healing. She became more receptive and 're-laxed', and did less self-injurious behaviours. She seemed happier in herself, and I felt the sessions were beneficial for her. She had co-oper-ated well. Jane left the school for an adult placement in July 2004.

Lucy, diagnosed with Velo-Cardio-Facial or Shprintzen Syndrome and epilepsy

Lucy was the youngest child that I had for healing, being aged seven at the time of the first session, and she had only been at the school for just over one month. I had a total of 56 healing sessions with Lucy over some six terms, spread over three school years, from 2002 to 2005.

Like some other pupils at the school she had an unusual medical diagnosis, namely, Chromosome 22 q 11 deletion, also known as Velo-Cardio-Facial Syndrome or Shprintzen Syndrome. When aged one year a heart murmur was noticed, and poor vocal sounding and a crooked smile led an alert registrar to diagnose this particular syndrome. Within her early years epileptic seizures began, her development regressed and she was said to be autistic. Now nearly 11 years old, she continues to require one-to-one care and supervision. Lucy still does not have any speech, but is a very aware and observant child. It is felt that epilepsy has been her main disabling problem.

Considering the total number of healing sessions which I have had with Lucy and the quantity of data available, I have had to be particularly selective in what can be shared here. However, I have tried my best to give you a characteristic picture of her various responses over the overall time period.

Session 1 – 9 October 2002

Lucy came with her main carer. She was making noises and was restless with her fingers, but also at times sat quietly. The session lasted about 15 minutes. We will see, in time, how she settles to this. Towards the end Lucy gave me a big open-mouthed smile and made good eye-to-eye contact.

After the two-week autumn half-term.

Session 4 – 6 November 2002

Lucy was fractious to begin with, and didn't want me to put my hands on her. However, quite quickly she relaxed and then allowed me to touch her. In fact she nearly went to sleep!

She sat on the chair throughout, with a carer nearby, and appeared quite happy.

Session 7 – 4 December 2002

I saw Lucy, without her carer sitting in today. She sat on the chair without any problem. However, she was restless most of the time with her fingers. Self-stimulating behaviours it seems. She sat there quite happily but did not, initially, want me to touch her. When I sat on a chair alongside her I could touch the stomach and back areas without objections. About 15 minutes today!

The written comments I received from Lucy's housemother for the autumn term made it clear that she had settled well into her home-life. Her eating had improved and overall there were less seizures, although when they did occur they were concentrated over one or two days and were then numerous.

After the Christmas holidays we had the first session of the spring term, the ninth in the series.

Session 9 – 16 January 2003

Lucy was quite restless today. Partly this was, perhaps, because she wasn't on the right sized chair. Eventually she sat on the very small chair in which her feet could be properly on the floor. But she is rather restless, in the sense of resisting and warding off physical contact. (Behaviours seen not just in the healing session.) I think it all belongs to her epileptic constitution. However, I expected that she do what I asked of her, and there were certainly times when she was much more receptive.

I think her energy needs balancing and calming through, and the incarnation harmonised.

Session 12 – 13 February 2003

Lucy was reluctant to leave her classroom to come with me. However, once in the healing room she was co-operative and quite happy. In fact she didn't reject me touching her at all today. She verbalised (sounded) quite a lot, and remained on her chair and did not attempt to get off. It was a positive, 15-minute session.

We continued, after the half-term break, to nearly mid-March.

Session 15 – 27 March 2003

She relaxed in the healing today. She doesn't resist, or push me away as she used to at the start of our sessions.

Written observations for the spring term from Lucy's class teacher noted certain changes in her behaviours including that, 'she seems more settled in the classroom environment and more confident', and 'when she is in good physical health (or as well as can be expected with Lucy), then she is a lot more cheerful and relaxed in school'. For the same term, her house-mother commented that, 'Lucy has been often unwell, which resulted in many fits. However, when well, and especially with those with whom she has a secure and realistic relationship, Lucy shows good co-operation and contact'.

    We then continued our sessions in the summer term, with the first one as follows.

Session 18 – 15 May 2003

In the healing session she was co-operative. Rather tired though. (She had a seizure last night around 10.30pm.) At one point she looked up at me and seemed happy, as she does in her delightful way.

    Lucy needs healing help to overcome her epilepsy. In fact this seems to be her main drawback which impedes her vitality and learning. She is nearly eight years old.

Session 22 – 2 July 2003

Lucy is usually, as today, rather fractious to start with. Trying to remove my hands from her shoulders and to get up off the chair. However, I expected that she should sit still and, when she realised that I meant what I said, she co-operated well. About ten minutes or so. I think the main problem is the epilepsy. She made very good and sustained eye-to-eye contact with me near the end of the session. Very direct.

I should point out that I believe that the initial uncooperativeness which Lucy often showed in the sessions was a characteristic of her epileptic constitution rather than of any rejection of healing *per se*.

After the long summer holidays we were ready to begin again in September. Before I resumed sessions with Lucy I spoke with her mother on the phone. She told me that Lucy had fits in the first week of the summer holiday but, after that, the holidays went very well. Lucy did lots of physical activities, swimming, long walks, trampolining. She also had a low carbohydrate diet with more meat and vegetables, and treatment for candida (a fungal infection of the gut).

Session 26 – 25 September 2003

Lucy came from the classroom for healing. At the beginning she was somewhat uncooperative, pushing my hands away, not wanting to be touched. However, she became more amenable. At one point she was fussing – crying/whining. However, one has to be firm with her as Lucy uses such strategies to get her own way. (We've seen this behaviour also on walks.) Quite a bit in the session she was banging her hand on her leg/knee. Is this a way of feeling more *in* herself perhaps?

Overall it was a good session and she became much more co-operative.

Session 27 – 2 October 2003

Saw Lucy for 10 or 15 minutes today. She co-operated well, though made a short fuss about sitting properly in the chair. She seems very well at present. Eating well. More vitality, much less tired.

Session 29 – 16 October 2003

As usual Lucy is whiny and resistant to sit properly in her chair for a time in the session. However, when I am clear what I expect of her she eventually complies. This behaviour is typical of Lucy in many situations and *is not special to healing*. I don't feel that she's rejecting healing *per se*.

We continued into December and started again after the Christmas break, in the New Year.

Session 32 – 15 January 2004

I took Lucy for healing today. However, after a short spell she did not want to sit in the chair, and resisted very actively and verbally (crying). This prolonged resistance I have never had before from her, and as it was clearly impossible to do anything constructive we finished the session after a short time.

Lucy behaved similarly in the following session and therefore I once again cut it short. From these experiences I decided to give healing a break with Lucy as nothing positive can be achieved without a child's willingness to be co-operative and receptive. Later I had four sessions in the summer term, when Lucy came with her main carer, and she then proved to be again willing and receptive.

Session 36 – 27 May 2004

Lucy came with N. again. She was sleepy at first. A positive session. Lucy co-operated and was receptive. She quite often turned her head to look at me. Works well with N. present. Lucy was actually warm today – hands and legs and feet. (She usually has cold hands.) She needs warmth.

I felt it would be good to continue healing with Lucy after the holidays in the new school year and see how she would respond. The first session was at the beginning of September.

Session 37 – 2 September 2004

Lucy came with a new carer called W. W. it transpired had experienced Reiki healing and asked if this was the same. I told her it was similar, and also in the course of the session told her about Lucy's main problem, i.e. uncontrolled epilepsy.

It was a good session. Lucy did not protest, and sat throughout in the small chair. She allowed touching.

I hope healing can help to alleviate her epilepsy; warm her through; and generally strengthen and build her up, also improve her immunity to illnesses. She still has no speech. Her hands are often cool. (Though at lunchtime today they were warm, i.e. after the healing session this morning.)

Session 39 – 13 September 2004

Lucy was accompanied by another new carer today who neither knows Lucy nor anything about healing. However, the session was fine.

Today, as in the other two sessions so far this term, Lucy is amenable to healing and she is not rejecting, protesting or whining. She allows me to touch her. She was lively in this session, not sleepy or floppy. She stamped her foot near the start; her left foot quite firmly on the floor. She also flicked her hands, rocked her head sideways at various times. She looked awake and 'with it'.

Lucy's housemother told me yesterday that she is much better than when we started term, and that she's also on new medication.

Session 41 – 23 September 2004

It was a good session. Lucy is receptive and not refusing healing contact. Lively and restless to begin, then becoming still and quiet. Hands warmer today, also her legs.

She has been keeping in good health the last two to three weeks I believe. Eats well, sleeps well. Not many fits at night. Has energy and is lively. Still not straight in posture, but better, and less lopsided than she was.

Session 44 – 7 October 2004

Lucy was very active in the session today. (I had a friend, B., from the university sitting in to observe.) Lucy was rocking, making sounds, etc. At one point when I was facing Lucy, and holding both her hands, she responded quite markedly – looking, smiling, laughing – B. remarked about this afterwards. Lucy's hands were cool. She stamped the floor vigorously with her left foot for a spell. She is receptive to hands-on healing and no longer initially rejects my hands touching her as she used to last school year.

Session 46 – 14 October 2004

Lucy became more lively in various ways once healing began. Moving and banging her left hand on her leg, rocking her head.

In this session I asked W. to sit on the stool behind Lucy whilst I was in front facing her. W. kept Lucy's head still and I held her hands in order to bring her, for a time, to stillness and quiet and to a centre. Lucy then looked at me, met my gaze, focused. I feel to bring her to stillness and peace and balance is important. She then also really smiled, even laughed and looked happy.

I made it a practice in the healing sessions to face Lucy, holding her hands and also holding her attention. This seemed definitely to help her to become more 'centred' and peaceful.

After the autumn half-term holiday I asked her housemother whether it had been all right. She said it had gone well with, apparently, no seizures. We resumed our sessions in November. Her housemother remarked that Lucy now *runs* energetically! It sounded as if things were changing markedly with her, probably, but perhaps not only, due to her changed anticonvulsant medication.

Session 52 – 22 November 2004

Another interesting 20-minute session with Lucy. She made quite a lot of repetitive noises at the start. Also moving more today than the two previous times, though not stamping her foot on the floor.

When I came in front of her and held her hands, she was peaceful and still and made eye contact and smiled. She is 'with it' when she comes to stillness and peace.

Lucy seems very well; no fits at all as far as I know. Looks happy to be in the session. Makes no attempt to get out or off the chair. At the end I asked her to stand up – which she did – and to open the door – which she did. I feel it's very positive with Lucy, and she seems in good shape.

W., the carer who had regularly sat in the sessions with Lucy through the autumn term, remarked in her notes dated 21 November 2004, 'It is really amazing how she has changed through the first half of the term and also after the half-term holidays'. She qualified this by pointing out that to begin with Lucy had struck her as a poor little child, living in a different world with no connection to the outside, and unable to do anything. Whereas, in contrast, her view of Lucy now was of a lovely and clever little girl who would return your smile when in a good mood, could express herself and could do tasks, e.g. making puzzles in school.

I also felt that I had had quite 'a journey' with Lucy through our 56 healing sessions and that the better control of her epileptic seizures, from autumn 2004, had certainly been a major turnaround for her general health and energy levels.

At this point I do wish to make it very clear that I am not in any way claiming that receiving spiritual healing is necessarily *the cause* of any progress which pupils have made. Where positive changes have been observed, by myself and others, it may well be that healing has contributed towards these, but there are also many other factors and interventions which need to be considered. The context in which the healing sessions took place was the therapeutic community setting, which is multi-faceted and holistic in nature. In Lucy's case, clear progress was seen after she had received a change of medication.

Nonetheless, in my review of practice in Chapter 7 I will certainly try to indicate clearly, out of my four years of experience in giving healing to pupils, in what overall ways spiritual healing *per se* does appear to have been beneficial and helpful, as evidenced through the actual healing sessions.

John, diagnosed with Fragile X Syndrome and within the autistic spectrum

John was 16 years old when I first took him for healing at the end of November 2002. This was the first of a total of 70 sessions with him over a three-year period.

John received a diagnosis of Fragile X Syndrome at two and a half years of age. As a tall young man he presented as fit and lean in build, with a clear-cut, well-formed, and good-looking face, but he was clearly very sensitive and shy towards his surroundings with a high, underlying anxiety level. He had long limbs and a smallish head. He was given to a lot of self-talk, but often found it difficult to relate to others and he had to have his own space. He had definite threshold problems in moving to different places and situations, and he needed a good deal of support from familiar others in order to cope with the demands of daily life. John had a particular fascination with mechanical things such as trains and diggers, and watching videos was a favourite recreational occupation. He tended to rush through most activities, as if he had no time to waste, and it was not easy for him to come to peace and quiet. When in a relaxed state he could reveal a good sense of humour, and he had a very likeable and pleasant personality. His behaviour was said to be 'within the Autistic Spectrum', and if he felt under pressure John could become very agitated, beating his chest with his fist, pushing others away, spitting and speaking loudly. He also has a rather itchy skin, with some dry patches, due to eczema. At least, fortunately, John was not epileptic.

Session 1 – 27 November 2002

Took John for the first time today. He came, at a rush, from basketwork. John sat on the chair, and he was quiet (no silly noises), and sat still. He is sensitive to being touched, and I worked from behind him. However, he was co-operative.

To create a space where John can just come to peace and quiet, and to be helped to 'get into himself' – this is my aim.

Session 2 – 4 December 2002

He came willingly from the rehearsal. Sat peaceful and still in the session, bent somewhat forward. No objection to my touching his shoulders, back and over his chest. A short, but good session.

Session 3 – 11 December 2002

John was bent over to start with but straightened up as the session went on. He allows touching, but it needs tuning in/responding to his wishes. Peaceful in the session. Afterwards he ran back to the hall.

We continued with healing after the Christmas holidays, in the New Year.

Session 4 – 20 January 2003

John came for healing from his classroom. He hurried, in his usual fashion, over to Chalice.

In the session he sat on the stool and was bent forwards. Eventually – towards the end – he straightened up more. He doesn't mind if I put my hands on his head or his back, but he's more sensitive about the front areas, e.g. over the chest, where he removed my hand after a short time.

However, I feel it is positive that he sits and co-operates as well as he does so far.

Session 7 – 10 February 2003

A very positive session. He sat up straight by himself for the first time. Not bent over as he has been before. John seemed relaxed and at ease.

Session 11 – 17 March 2003

He was willing to come, and co-operative in the session. Will sit up when asked to. Tolerates touch now on the chest area. (In the house he does a lot of talking to himself but doesn't usually use personal pronouns, such as 'I', 'me', 'my', etc.)

Session 14 – 7 April 2003

He comes readily to the session. Sits up straight on request. Quiet and co-operative. At the end he departs quickly!

John tends to do everything quickly, but also there is the threshold 'stuckness' and hesitancy. A happy 'middle', in between the extremes, is not easy for him.

(Today at breakfast, 8 April, he was self-talking a lot. He's not contained 'in himself' sufficiently, but flowing out in language.)

The written feedback I received both from John's housemother and his teacher for the spring term, from January to April, sounded positive.

His housemother wrote that John was more settled and less tense, more co-operative and less stuck and noisy.

His teacher reported that John is more relaxed than ever before and his moods are more even, with an increase in 'direct' interactions with others.

We resumed healing after the Easter break. His holidays at home seem to have gone well.

Session 15 – 12 May 2003

John came from weaving in the classroom. He was quiet and co-operative, and he sits up when I ask him to.

Last term there were several occasions, in the house-setting, when he did use personal pronouns, e.g. 'my', 'I'. However, I believe he needs help with coming to the self-identity experience and in centring himself.

Session 21 – 7 July 2003

His eyes are a bit red. He suffers from hay fever. Yesterday John had a day at the beach and he stood most of the time, away from the others, watching what was going on.

John was a bit sensitive with the healing today and he removed my hand several times from his back and chest areas. But he's basically co-operative and quiet.

In various situations John was often very restless in his body and could, for example, hardly stand still when the house community stood in a circle for morning and evening 'prayers'. This behaviour contrasted with his stillness in our healing sessions.

The new school year began in September 2003, and I spoke with John's parents after they had brought him back to school. His mother said they had had a good holiday with John and that he had been more relaxed than usual. Also he had been no trouble in coming back to school! His housemother also reported that there had been no spitting or throwing things around when John returned. So, a smooth transition!

John continued to be co-operative and receptive in our healing sessions throughout the autumn term, and was able to sit still without fidgeting. After the fortnight half-term holiday he returned to school, again without any fusses or drama. After Christmas we had the first session of 2004.

Session 32 – 12 January 2004

John was a bit slow to leave class and come with me – but he did.

In the session he was co-operative. He sat upright and was still and quiet. However, he was not keen to have my hands touching his chest or abdomen areas for very long, and he indicated this by removing them gently. (He is rather tense and noisy in the house at the moment – still settling back to school.)

John continued, as usual, to co-operate well in the sessions in the spring term and also the summer term that year.

His summer holidays at home went well for the first two weeks and he was on the whole very co-operative. Unfortunately a family bereavement took place, and this changed the usual patterns of life at home for John and led to some unsettlement. He reacted very strongly, and negatively, to a visit to a local college. His eczema seemed worse that summer. However, we made a good start with our healing sessions in the autumn.

Session 42 – 2 September 2004

John co-operated well in healing. He has been somewhat tense in the house, and quite noisy with his self-talk. However, in the session he was quiet and sat still and allowed direct touching; also on his chest. So this certainly provided him with a quiet space.

Session 45 – 13 September 2004

John came to Chalice brought by his helper, M., from Cinnabar (the seniors building). Seemingly he had been disturbed by another pupil.

Anyway he co-operated in the session, though was more bent over than sometimes. I asked him to sit up and he did become less bent then!

John does need help to come to real inner peace in which he may find himself better. (Tomorrow he goes to another Camphill place, a further education college, for a three-day trial period.)

Session 47 – 30 September 2004

John was quiet today. However, he gently indicated that he didn't want my hands on his body too long. I respected his wishes and, for example, held my hands on either side of his neck without touching.

The half-term break came towards the end of October, and apparently the holidays were generally all right at home.

Session 52 – 8 November 2004

As another pupil had been late coming for healing I had a shorter session with John than normal.

He came in and sat on the stool while I finished making some notes. In the healing John indicated that he didn't want my hands on his back (eczema?), by gently removing them. I acknowledged his wishes. He is I think very sensitive. However, I didn't have the impression that he didn't want, or wasn't willing, to be here. Indeed at the end when I had finished and also switched the music off, he remained sat on the stool. He was not in a rush to leave!

In healing he sits quietly and is not restless. Although not completely still, his feet and legs, otherwise often in movement, *are* still.

Session 54 – 22 November 2004

John sat quietly for healing. He didn't mind when I touched his shoulders and head, but with his back and chest areas indicated that he didn't want me to touch these areas – at least not for long – by gently moving my hand away.

When I come in front of him and put my hands on his feet, he bends over and covers his face with his hands – seemingly very shy. So it's easier for him when I rather stand *behind* him.

That John sits still and quietly in the session is itself an achievement. He can be so restless and ill at ease in other settings.

He still seems to have a bit of a cold and a runny nose. When I look at him he meets my gaze fleetingly but doesn't hold it. When I said it was time to go he got up quickly, took his book and video, and went out. Light-footedly he goes back to class, almost skipping as he does.

Session 55 – 29 November 2004

John indicated today that basically he didn't want me to make physical contact with him. He makes this known by moving my hands away in a gentle but clear gesture and manner.

I respected this and moved my own hands accordingly, keeping them rather at a distance from his body, i.e. non-contact healing.

On the whole John comes to stillness (not absolute of course!), and quietness (also not absolute), in the sessions. For a person so sensitive and often so restless and uncomfortable, this does provide a space for him to come more to peace.

Session 56 – 6 December 2004

I didn't have the music on today, but still I cannot say it was a silent session! John was self-verbalising, but not all the time and not loudly.

He seemed quite happy and when I had my hands on his feet and then looked up, he was smiling.

To help bring John into an experience of bodily stillness and inner peacefulness – even if only for five minutes – would, I think, be a healing experience.

John continued to have healing in the spring term and the start of the summer term. It was my policy to work with him and respect his wishes as an 18-year-old young man and whenever he indicated that I move, or remove, my hands from a certain position I did so. Given that understanding, John was co-operative and receptive. I kept the sessions undemanding and as relaxed as I could. I had also newly put a wall mirror into the room so that John, and other pupils, could see themselves reflected in it. A new year arrived.

Session 58 – 24 January 2005

I saw John this morning. We had plenty of time so there was no need to rush.

It was an unusual session because I entered into conversation with him. This was through me asking him questions and he giving me answers.

John had been speaking about 'coaches', one, two or three I think. I asked him where the coaches were. 'A railway station.' I asked him if he liked to go on a train; and who with. I asked him about his house, garden, what his father did and so on.

I had the clear impression that John *understood* what I was asking and that he could answer. I spoke very quietly and in an undemanding way.

He allowed me to put my hands on him, though again at certain times he did remove them and then I rather just moved them through the space around him.

At times he sat pretty still and he seemed quite happy with the healing, not strained or stressed. Smiling sometimes. Overall it felt peaceful and relaxed.

It did, however, seem by John's behaviours in other situations, such as in school and in the house, that he was feeling under some stress and pressure during the spring term. He had a new teacher from January 2005 and perhaps he felt over-stretched. For example, he missed one healing session because he was 'on the floor' in Cinnabar and refusing to move. However, I don't believe that this was because he was averse to having healing. Indeed just before the spring half-term I asked John if he wanted to carry on or stop having healing. He couldn't give me a clear answer but as far as I could judge it he seemed generally comfortable with the sessions, and I knew from the house side that if John did *not* want to do something he would make this very clear by saying, 'I not'. He had become more self-assertive. We therefore continued with the sessions.

Session 67 — 14 March 2005

John had what I would describe as a 'good' healing session. He was calm and at ease. Talking to himself quietly at times. Co-operative and receptive. As usual he indicated when he wanted me to remove my hands, but I was allowed to keep them over his chest/back areas for quite a long time today.

He doesn't mind when I put my hands on his feet, and I asked him if he could tell me 'how it felt'. He said, 'Very nice'. (This is a phrase he comes out with in various circumstances and situations.)

Actually *before* I began healing today I asked John if this was all right for him and he said, 'Very nice'.

Although he is very sensitive and shy I have the impression he likes healing, generally speaking.

In May we had our final session, Number 70! Looking back over all these sessions with John I had seen that he could come, again and again, to a clear measure of stillness and quiet in healing and, I hoped, also to some real inner peace.

Considering that he was someone who through his special constitution so often displayed restlessness, rather as if he has put on a hair shirt at the start of each new day, it was impressive and important that he could come to relative peace and quiet in our sessions. John had made progress in his personal development and was now more able to express his needs and wishes verbally and to make choices for himself.

He left the school that summer to go on to a Camphill further education college.

Tracey, diagnosed with epilepsy and autistic behaviours

This special young lady had had a difficult start into earthly life. It seems she had epilepsy from birth onwards, was on a life-support machine and, when eventually dismissed from hospital, her parents were given a very bleak prognosis: hearing nil, sight nil. However, through intensive and prolonged sensory stimulation Tracey reacted in such a way that it became evident that she could both see and hear, and slow progress was made. By the time she was around 12 years old she was described as having severe learning difficulties, autistic behavioural characteristics, and epilepsy which had been stabilised by medication. One of the most striking things about her appearance was her walking on tiptoe and not putting her heels on the ground. She was a good-looking girl with a rounded face and a largish head.

Tracey was very self-willed and could be very stubborn. Any aggressive tendencies she had were more of a self-defensive nature than actively directed towards others. Generally she did not like to be touched and was very sensitive, especially to noise. However, Tracey had made some good progress at the school when I first took her for healing sessions in May 2002. She was then 15 and had already had the great benefit of individual eurythmy therapy. Tracey unfortunately had no speech.

Session 1 – 8 May 2002

Tracey came in the afternoon at the end of break with K., her helper. She didn't object to me being behind her and having my hands close to her head and back. However, she made it clear that she doesn't allow me, yet, to directly touch her hands or legs. She did clap onto my hand, but that was *her* wish and initiative.

So a good start, but hopefully Tracey will gradually allow more contact. I believe she needs help to incarnate further and to draw into herself.

Session 2 – 15 May 2002

I do not put any pressure on her. My only expectation is that she will sit on the chair for healing – which she does. She is very sensitive but allows me to have my hands close to her and, at times, actually touching – especially the back area. Towards the end of the session I could also put my hand gently on her knees.

She needs incarnating into her limbs. Makes a lot of 'astral' movements with arms and hands 'out and about'. No speech but makes noises. Larynx area needs working on.

Note: By 'astral' movements I mean bodily movements, but which are not directed and controlled by her ego – her individual inner being.

Session 3 – 22 May 2002

This was a particularly interesting session. I let Tracey direct it largely, in as much as *she* took my hands and directed them. She was calm and also happy it seems, by the sounds she made and the expression on her face.

Tracey is open for healing on her terms and I in no way impose my will over hers, but aim to work with her.

Session 4 – 29 May 2002

Another very interesting session with Tracey, this time without K. present as she was needed elsewhere.

As before I let Tracey direct the session. She can take my hands and decide where to put them. A number of times she actually put my hands to her face. When she takes both my hands at once – that is when I'm standing behind her – she uses them with symmetrical co-ordination and movements. So, a co-operative and 'mutually agreeable' session.

Interestingly, Tracey's housemother at the school told me that Tracey was better in the house since the healing started.

Session 5 – 12 June 2002

An interesting session, with Tracey again taking the initiative to direct my hands. At times she was very energetic, moving her hands, and mine, very vigorously! At one point she got very excited, shaking herself. In the session she seemed happy – laughing at times.

I feel it's positive, and I hope that she receives benefit in whatever way she needs it (which *her* inner being knows better than I!).

Session 7 – 26 June 2002

Tracey came again today. As usual she directed my hands. However, as the session wore on I was also allowed to put my hands on her independently, without her 'taking charge'.

It remains to be seen how the healing may help her. I feel that a main thing is to help to 'centre' her and to draw her into her body. She doesn't allow me to touch her legs/knees, in contrast to her upper body.

Session 8 – 3 July 2002

I took Tracey along without K. today. A good session. She also *did* let me touch her legs, at least at times. So this is a change. I feel overall to help her to come 'into herself', to 'centre' her, is my aim.

Tracey's housemother reported for the summer term 2002 that, 'She is more calm and she is not pulling people so often'.

After the summer holidays I resumed sessions with Tracey in September. According to her housemother the holidays at home had been difficult, with tempers, wetting and soiling. Back at the school though things were going all right in the house-setting.

Session 9 – 4 September 2002

She was similar today as before the holidays, taking my hands during the session. However, I could also put hands on without Tracey always taking and holding them, i.e. she tolerates some direct touch from me. She seemed cheerful.

The planned tenth session on 11 September actually didn't take place. This was because in spite of some help from her teacher to point her in the right direction, Tracey didn't wish to come with me to Chalice. I had no intention, of course, of making her come against her will, and so that was that. In fact after this I must have decided to give healing a break with Tracey for that autumn term, and only resumed in Spring 2003.

Session 10 – 6 February 2003

I had a session with Tracey today – the first since early September. (Her teacher thought it was a good idea to take her for healing again.) Well, she accepts healing on her terms, and will allow me to touch her when she is willing – but certainly not always! Sometimes she takes my hands and puts them quite firmly to her, e.g. on her face. I work with *her* degree of willingness.

Session 11 – 13 February 2003

I had to fetch Tracey from the classroom today as I hadn't been there at break-time. She came willingly with me, just placing her hand on my shoulder. She walks down the steps to Chalice skilfully, on tiptoe, and with alternate foot placements.

In the session Tracey was co-operative, at times taking my hands to direct them, but at other times allowing me to gently place my hands on her, e.g. on her shoulders and along her spine. She seemed quite happy and, at one point, she was laughing.

At the end of the session she went back with me to her classroom.

Three more sessions were possible after the week's half-term break.

Session 12 – 6 March 2003

An interesting session today!

I let her sit where she wanted, on chairs rather than the stool. She allowed me to eventually touch her knees and legs today! I first kept a little distance away, but then could also make direct hands-on contact.

Tracey seemed fine in the session and, afterwards, she was less up on her toes walking than I've often seen.

Session 13 – 20 March 2003

An interesting session with Tracey. She allows me to touch her legs now, which she never used to do. She seems very cheerful in the session. As usual *she* directs my hands part of the time.

Session 14 – 27 March 2003

She is much more tolerant of me touching her than she used to be. Today she hardly directed my hands at all. I can also touch her legs without her objecting much. She always looks cheerful.

I had some interesting written feedback from Tracey's teacher for this spring term. He reported that she was becoming more focused than ever before, showing far greater involvement with her surroundings and peers. She is, he wrote, 'more grounded'. She was also making more eye contact, and showed more desire to be involved in certain activities.

I must of course again hasten to add that it would be much too simplistic to attribute these very good developments directly to the healing input. There were many other inputs to consider in Tracey's experience at the school and within 'the total therapeutic community'. Still, all this was very encouraging and after the Easter break we continued.

Session 15 – 15 May 2003

Tracey came today. The session went well. At times she got very excited, rocking back and forth. Also laughing. She allowed me to put my hands on her knees etc., and though she did take my hands off at times, I was left more free to go where I thought fit.

Still no speech, and she is movement disturbed and walks on her toes. She didn't actually look directly at me, so no real eye-to-eye contact. She needs to centre more, and gain more control over her body. But Tracey is quite a personality and a force to reckon with, especially if crossed!

Session 17 – 25 June 2003
She came to healing today quite willingly. She was fine in the session, though I have to be guided by what she is willing to go along with.

In the new school year, after the long summer holidays, we resumed our healing work.

Session 19 – 11 September 2003
Took Tracey for healing. On the way to Chalice she stopped at the steps going down, and turned around and went back in the direction of the school. However, we then came back, this time avoiding the steps.

She was fine in the session – co-operative and allowing me to put my hands on her. Today she did not take my hands firmly (as she used to), and direct me. I was allowed to have more free rein. A positive session.

Session 20 – 18 September 2003
I fetched Tracey from the classroom. She came with me in her own time. Co-operative in the session. Seemed happy. At times she got quite excited, moving her arms rapidly. She allows me to touch her and is more tolerant of this than she used to be.

Her teacher says she is 'more focused' and is getting on well.

Session 22 – 2 October 2003
An interesting session. She came with me willingly and is co-operative. But I have to 'tune in' with her and go with her 'signals' and communication. She seemed relaxed and to enjoy the session. Good eye-to-eye contact, direct and focused.

Then after the two-week autumn half-term.

Session 23 – 13 November 2003

Tracey was not very willing to let me touch her *lightly* today for healing. She was not in a bad mood, but just not letting me keep my hands in one place for very long. She was, however, cheerful enough. I then decided simply to touch her with *more pressure* and she allowed this! This was then more like a body-geography awareness exercise. This went well.

Session 24 – 20 November 2003

In the session, as last week, I did some *firm* touch on her limbs – arms and legs – and also her back. She completely tolerated this, and seemed quite happy and co-operative. These were really incarnating downward gestures and movements through touch.

Session 25 – 27 November 2003

An interesting session!

I decided it was best to apply firm touch pressure, so to speak, from head to foot. And she *does* allow this – even with me pressing very firmly on her head and face. I think she needs this to make her more aware of her bodily boundaries.

Actually when I had my hands on her face, and she was facing me also, there was much more eye-to-eye contact possible. So the session was more of a lower-sense stimulation (i.e. through touch and movement), than healing *per se*, but I felt this was positive and good for her.

Session 26 – 4 December 2003

Essentially I had another lower-sense session with Tracey to which she responded very well. Through firm touch pressure helping her to experience her body. Of course *not* touching her frontal areas at all. I also stamped her feet on the floor, and clapped her two hands together. She seemed very happy in the session, and was laughing sometimes.

The remaining sessions that I had with Tracey were all along the same lines and directed and intended to strengthen her own self-experience through greater body awareness. I did, however, realise that I had now moved beyond the remit of spiritual healing. In order to continue to have individual sessions with Tracey I therefore felt I needed to have her parents' new consent for lower-sense and body-geography exercises in place of healing. I wrote to them to request this but, unfortunately, I did not receive a reply. I tried one further healing session with Tracey in the summer term 2004, but it was clear to me that lower-sense exercises (see Woodward and Hogenboom 2002) would be much more relevant to her needs at this stage and therefore I did not continue healing.

So this had been for me a very interesting and surprising 'journey' with Tracey in which, from being someone very sensitive to being touched, she had progressed to accepting hands-on healing and then benefiting I believe from very firm and direct touch experiences. Perhaps the healing work had made this new development possible for her.

A school report in January 2004 noted that in the last year Tracey had become much more comfortable with bodily contact, which was seen as a very important breakthrough for someone who previously could not bear to be touched unless it was at her own initiation. It seemed the more physical her relationship with others, the more involved and aware she became and, I think one could add, that she was also then more centred and focused in herself. Curatively, this can be described as progress both in her incarnation into her own body and into the surrounding social world.

Sandra, diagnosed with Autistic Spectrum Disorder

While to a large extent Tracey herself had directed and controlled the healing sessions which I had with her, Sandra by contrast simply accepted the healing and, so to speak, 'soaked it up like a sponge' as we shall see shortly.

Sandra was in foster care from birth and was deprived of any early stimulation, but within the first year she was taken on by her close relatives, who were later given guardianship responsibility. At around two and a half years of age she received an initial diagnosis of Autistic Spectrum Disorder. Sandra was very late in giving affection towards others, beginning only around age seven. She showed impairments in communication, social interaction and imaginative play. Behavioural difficulties partly due to her frustration at her communication problems could arise, such as hitting out at peers and also some self-injurious behaviours, including head butting. She was very sensitive to noise, very musical and also very insecure. There was gaze avoidance and little or no use of eye-to-eye contact. Speech was limited with some echolalia. She liked order and routine and was rather obsessional and impulsive. Diet was very limited and of her own choice. However, Sandra was described as 'a happy, loving girl who is eager to learn'. She had actually done very well in her relatively short time at the school. Physically Sandra was very able and liked walking, running and swimming, but had no sense of danger!

I began spiritual healing with Sandra in the autumn term 2005 in late September and, from the first session onwards, she proved to be very co-operative and very receptive. Because Sandra's behaviour and responses were so consistent from session to session, only a comparatively small selection from the total of 20 sessions given over two school terms will now be included here. No background music was used and this enhanced the peace and quiet of this special time and space in the day.

Session 1 – 26 September 2005

This first session with Sandra went very well! She co-operated throughout, and I told her what I was going to do with my hands before I did it.

She allowed me to put my hands on her shoulders, standing behind her. From there I went to her head (very lightly). Then I sat on the left-hand chair and put my hands along her spine – base and neck. Then to her heart area, over at the front and touching at the back. I did not of course intend to put my left hand touching her upper chest and kept it at a distance, but she took my hand and pressed it to her chest. I then withdrew it again to a slight distance. I then went down on my knees in front of her, to place my hands on her feet.

At one point Sandra bent down to put the thin Velcro straps on her right shoe in the correct place; to put it exactly right!

From this position I stood up and went back to stand behind Sandra, hands on her shoulders again. I finished the healing by moving my hands above and downwards over her head and through her energy field three times.

Sandra had appeared entirely comfortable with the session. At no point had she wished to get up off the stool, nor did she show any objection to being touched. It had been a quiet, peaceful, session. However, I wondered if this was a 'honeymoon' session in which she was so co-operative and well-behaved. Would it be the same on Wednesday? The whole session was not more than 15 minutes.

Session 2 – 28 September 2005

A very orderly and peaceful session. Sandra is totally co-operative and sits still and, mainly, quietly on the stool. She did some self-talking in the session. She seems quite happy with the healing and does not at all object to me touching her. I was able to go through all the normal hands-on procedure, i.e. starting on shoulders; on head; along spine; over the heart; solar plexus; on feet; 'top and tail' (i.e. one hand on her head and the other on the base of her spine); and finishing with moving my hands from above her head and downwards three times.

Sandra seems to me very receptive to receiving healing. Interestingly when I had my hands on her feet and then looked up towards her she didn't look directly at me; rather avoiding eye contact. She strikes me as quite a large-headed, 13-year-old, young lady.

Session 3 – 3 October 2005

It was a very peaceful session. Sandra was again entirely co-operative and receptive throughout.

She allows hands-on contact; though just once when I had my right hand on her back (corresponding to the solar plexus area), and my left hand on the solar plexus area, she did remove my right hand. I went along with her wish. Otherwise I was able to follow the normal hands-on positions procedure.

I didn't talk to Sandra in the session apart from to say 'well done' at one point, as I wanted to maintain the peaceful and still mood. When I had my hands on her feet she was leaning forwards and blew my hair. I didn't react to this at all. However, I did look up towards her later when I still had my hands on her feet but there was no direct eye-to-eye contact between us.

Through the session Sandra sat with her hands together, giving a very 'contained' and 'together' impression, and she showed no inclination to get off the stool until we had finished.

I felt that Sandra was 'the perfect healee' as she was so very receptive and our subsequent sessions continued in the same ordered and peaceful manner. In the fifth session when I had my hands on her feet and then looked up at her she was smiling, looked happy and made for the first time direct eye-to-eye contact with me. This was repeated also in the next session, which was the last one before the autumn half-term break. Actually in that sixth session with Sandra I had noticed that her lower spine area, which up to then had always felt rather cool, was now warm.

Sandra's housemother reported that since the healing sessions had started in the first half of the autumn term, there had been no incidents of challenging or bizarre behaviours and that Sandra was noticeably less reactionary. Yes, one weekend there had been a few occasions of *attempted* pinching, hitting and head butting but, overall, big changes had been seen with her compared to the first few weeks of term. Her teacher also reported that healing appeared to have a calming influence on Sandra and that she had had good weeks in school during the period of the twice-weekly healing sessions.

Her guardian reporting on the two weeks half-term holiday at home wrote that, 'Over the last two weeks I have noted Sandra seems to be more patient and prepared to put up with people generally'.

We resumed our sessions in November.

Session 7 — 14 November 2005

Sandra co-operated well throughout. She was more animated than in previous sessions, not so still, quiet and peaceful perhaps? However, this was the first session after a two-week half-term and actually the first one for a month or so since the last session.

She again allowed me to go through the sequence of hand positions and did not mind being touched. I felt her lower back as cool. She was speaking, sounding, singing, at various times. She spontaneously kissed my left hand when it was over her heart area. When I went to her feet she blew on my head and also kissed my head! In these ways *she* was making contact with me.

At the end I said, 'well done' and told her I would see her again on Wednesday that week. She seemed perfectly happy to be having healing again.

Actually when I had been in front of her at her feet, she had pointed to my eyes. Also at the end she referred to eyes again and pointed to her eyes. This was new.

We continued with our sessions. I felt warmth at her lower spine instead of coolness; there was more direct eye-to-eye contact; and she continued to be completely receptive. The twelfth session was the last one for us before the Christmas holidays.

Session 12 – 30 November 2005

Another good session with Sandra. Good in the sense that she is receptive and co-operative and appears to be comfortable with the healing, as shown by her willingness and her smiles at certain points, e.g. when I look up at her when I'm at her feet or when I sit next to her at the end of the session.

Sandra is not 'turned away' as she used to be, and I feel there is good contact between us.

I did all the usual hand positions. She didn't speak, apart from when she came in and at the end. I don't feel that coolness at the base of her spine as I used to. How were her feet placed? When I saw her feet they were flat on the floor.

Towards the end (after the feet position), when she was still bent over and I was ready for 'top and tail', I asked Sandra to sit up. She did not do so immediately, but did a short time later, and she also repeated what I'd said to her.

Today was the last session this term. I asked her if she liked healing. Her reactions suggested that she did – she smiled. I said I'd see her next term, after the holidays.

A written report from Sandra's housemother for this second half of the autumn term described that Sandra had got on very well in the house-setting, apart from two incidents which had been triggered by definite causes. Interestingly there had also been a definite improvement with her diet – no Marmite! Ate lettuce! Her teacher reported that Sandra went happily to healing sessions and returned from them calmly. A new development was that Sandra had started to join the other children out in the playground at break-time, whereas previously she had stayed inside, because of the likelihood of some aggressive behaviours from her towards her peers.

From the three-week Christmas holidays at home Sandra's guardian wrote to me, 'Lots of people have commented on how calm and relaxed Sandra is. I too have seen this. She is just as loving and mischievous as she always was, but there is that air of almost dignity. It has been a good three weeks'.

In the New Year and the spring term we resumed but only managed to have four out of the planned six sessions. She had missed three sessions due to illness but we were able to fit in one extra session. In fact Sandra had been ill with a temperature for three days and stayed in bed without stirring. This was most unusual, and therefore significant, as Sandra had never really been ill before. However, we did get one session in before her illness, the thirteenth in the series.

Session 13 – 16 January 2006

A good healing session with Sandra. She co-operated throughout. There was also warm contact between us, through eye contact, smiles and speech. I went through the full range of hand positions. When I had my hand over her heart area she kissed it, however, she didn't blow or kiss my head today when I was at her feet. There was warmth on the lower spine. She didn't speak during the healing itself, but sat quiet and peacefully. At the start she said 'Let's try', and I affirmed, 'Let's try and have a healing session'.

The most striking thing in this session was the open, friendly, contact between us.

When Sandra recovered from her illness we had three more good, positive sessions before the spring half-term break. Sandra's housemother commented at half-term that Sandra was using more language and was less insular, and *she felt instinctively that healing had helped her but could not define how.* At home for a week her guardian, as usual, kept to a clear pattern and routine for Sandra and he reported that, 'There is nothing I can put my finger on but her whole attitude seems to be more confident. She certainly is happy'.

After the half-term we again only managed to have four of the planned six healing sessions. She missed the last two times because of a recurrence of her fluey symptoms. But those we did have continued in the same vein as all the previous ones, with complete co-operation, receptivity, relaxation and increased warm contact between us.

Whilst once again I have to point out that healing was not the only factor that may have contributed to the good progress seen with Sandra over the two terms in which our sessions took place, the feedback received from others is, I believe, clearly indicative of the likely benefit from healing *per se*. And not least of course was the positive feedback received from Sandra herself in the sessions, especially in the form of increased interpersonal contact and warmth.

On this very positive note, I will close this chapter so that we can now take a well-earned 'breather' before describing how other children with special needs responded individually to spiritual healing in my sessions with them.

CHAPTER 5

Healing Sessions II

Simon, diagnosed with autistic features and emotional and behavioural difficulties

Simon was diagnosed as having 'autistic features' in that he needed a consistent, structured and predictable routine during the school day. He had very poor language and communication skills and marked emotional and behavioural difficulties. At times his behaviour could be very challenging, and sometimes violent, putting both himself and others at risk. He had a high anxiety level and because of this he was also very vulnerable. His attention span was very short and he could be very restless, and he had severe learning difficulties. On the other hand Simon had a very likeable and endearing personality and he could show care and consideration towards other children. He arrived at the school in the summer term 2004 and I first took him for individual healing sessions in September of that year when he was 12 years old.

Session 1 – 6 September 2004

Simon was brought to Chalice for healing. He came in and I showed him where to sit – on the stool. I had just a short session with him, 10 to 15 minutes. On the whole he co-operated well. At times he wanted to lie on the chair next to the stool, but I expected him to sit up.

Simon didn't attempt to run off at all and he allowed hands-on touch.

He has some speech and he asked for a drink. For the first session, and the first time to meet me, he did quite well.

His face looked rather 'unformed' and didn't look 'penetrated' by his ego. His hands were very warm. Hopefully when he gets used to coming he'll manage to sit for longer and come to peace.

Session 2 – 13 September 2004

I saw Simon again today. On the whole he was fairly co-operative but I had to exercise a clear level of expectation with him as otherwise he would have taken advantage. He was 'trying out' what he could get away with.

However, I insisted that he sit up on the stool and listen to the music rather than chatter.

He allowed hands-on touch and, at times, he sat very still and was receptive. In between he would flop! He is a likeable fellow with a rather cheeky look and smile. He gives me the impression of lacking form, outwardly and inwardly.

Session 3 – 20 September 2004

Simon was sitting well and was co-operative for most of the session, but restless and flopping about towards the end. However, I insisted he co-operate in order to finish properly, which he did. A friendly but impulsive boy.

Session 4 – 27 September 2004

He was very good in healing today. Sat up, still, and quiet, and peaceful for about 10 to 15 minutes. Not restless at all, nor flopping about.

Session 5 – 11 October 2004

He came across with me from the end of the afternoon school break.

Simon was well-behaved throughout the session. No very impulsive movements, no flopping over. He referred to seeing his father at the weekend. He was well-together I would say. Sat, quietly, still, and was peaceful.

Session 6 – 14 October 2004

In the session he co-operated well – mainly. He sat still and allowed hands-on touching.

I had to ask him to keep his head still at one point and also to listen to the music instead of speaking but, overall, he managed well and complied.

Simon is impulsive and near the end of the session he moved quickly off the stool and opened the lid of a wooden box which was part of the furniture in the room. However, I sat him down again to finish properly.

He's a character, a friendly chap.

Session 7 – 21 October 2004

Simon was rather restless and impulsive today, getting off the stool several times in the session. However, he generally co-operates well. He said some things repeatedly, e.g. referring to the rain. He's a friendly, warm person though and very likeable.

With this achieved, we had arrived at the start of the fortnight autumn half-term. I carried on with Simon then in November, and he continued to be co-operative and receptive in healing. Some further examples of this follow.

Session 10 – 22 November 2004

Simon was quiet and co-operative. Not as impulsive with sudden movements as he used to be. He knows me and comes willingly after the afternoon break-time and he goes back to his classroom quietly and properly after the session with me accompanying him.

Simon did speak a few times in the session, but not speaking *to me* to communicate, rather just coming out with odd things just as his movements can be sometimes. Seems 'happy' in the session – I mean quite content to be here.

Session 12 – 2 December 2004

Simon came running across with a co-worker. He was out of breath when he sat down.

He managed well. I had to ask him to put his feet down a number of times, rather than to sit cross-legged. He complied at once. Just ten minutes today.

After the Christmas holidays we carried on in the New Year.

Session 13 – 20 January 2005

I had a good session with Simon, 15 to 20 minutes. Most of the time he sat still and quietly. Once or twice he got off the stool, i.e. spontaneously stood up, but he was quite willing to sit down again when I made it clear we hadn't finished.

It was quite impressive how quiet and co-operative Simon was. He did speak a little to himself at times but I didn't really grasp what he said. I think

it's just thoughts that go through his mind which he verbalises, but not necessarily with any clear thread to them.

In appearance Simon lacks *form*. I think he needs *'containing'*, i.e. helping him to centre more *in* himself. Coming to peace and quiet can help this
process.

Session 14 – 27 January 2005

Simon had a healing session for about 20 minutes. He was mainly quiet, still
and co-operative. He got up off the stool once, but sat down again when I
guided him back onto it. He talked, rather spoke repeatedly, from time to
time about 'The Bill' (a TV programme), just repeating the words.

After the healing sessions, since I needed to hang on to him until
break-time, I asked him to do some copied writing, which he did very well
indeed.

I continued to have healing sessions with Simon during that spring term and
after the actual sessions he remained in the room, where he did some copied
writing and form-drawing exercises. This arrangement worked well and was
in place owing to certain teaching shortages at that time.

Session 16 – 7 February 2005

Simon was co-operative. He noticed the colours on the wall cast by the sun-
light shining through the coloured glass.

I think if healing helps to bring Simon into more peace, quiet, stillness,
then he can be helped to come more 'to himself' – to be more centred.

Afterwards we did some writing and simple form drawing. He doesn't
naturally do the 'crossing over' in drawing loops or figure eights, but I take
his hand to help him to do this.

Session 19 – 28 February 2005

Very quiet and peaceful session with Simon today. He's very co-operative
and receptive. No impulsive movements today at all. Perfectly happy to
receive touch.

We do writing and form drawing after healing, both to help his concentration and to centre him.

We continued into March and then started again in the summer term, after
the three-week holiday.

Session 25 – 25 April 2005

Saw Simon today – the first time this term. He was a little restless, but he was co-operative. At times in the session he was very still and quiet. I don't speak much with Simon as I feel that peace, stillness and quiet are the most important things for him. When we finished healing, after 20 minutes, I delivered him to his teacher for the painting lesson.

Session 27 – 9 May 2005

Simon was quite restless at times today, but also still and quiet in between.

What does he need? What's his problem? Impulsivity, distractiveness. He sits with his soles turned up from the floor. I asked him to put his shoes on the floor, which he did. I feel he's not grounded enough, not connecting properly with the earth. He has a characteristic of touching the bottom of his shoes with his hands. He needs centering and grounding; incarnating.

Overall it was a positive session and he co-operated.

This was then the last session which I had with Simon in the school year 2004–2005.

When Simon had come to the school in May 2004 he had had poor communication, aggression and outbursts, was hyperactive and very anxious. He was sometimes kicking, head butting and pinching others. His subsequent progress over the school year was described in his school and house reports as 'remarkable'. He had become settled, relaxed, happy, affectionate and charming. He was still obsessed with routines, but his expressive speech and communication had improved and he appeared to be getting more of a sense of himself, was more sociable and he was able to relate better to others. Clearly the predictable routine, structures and clear expectations of the school, as a therapeutic environment, had been greatly to Simon's benefit.

Five months later I was able to have a further 17 healing sessions with Simon in the course of the new school year, making a total of 44. He had grown much taller over the long summer holidays and clearly puberty was fast approaching.

In the six sessions which took place with Simon before the autumn half-term he came willingly to all the sessions and he could be completely still at times. He allowed hands-on contact though sometimes he also appeared to test out to see what reactions he might get from squeezing my hands, or touching my head if I was at his feet. I had learnt from experience that it was important not to react to any impulsive movements Simon made but to remain very calm and collected.

After the first few sessions I decided that it was better to work from behind Simon, as this was less distracting for him, and allowed a greater opportunity for him to come to some peace and stillness.

After the two weeks of half-term which his father described as, 'went well, with only three incidents of violence', we had another series of six sessions, and I again worked from behind him. Simon continued to be co-operative to receive hands-on healing; he sat on the stool well, only getting up once in most sessions; he no longer explored and 'checked out' the room as he had before half-term; and there were hardly any impulsive movements and longer periods of stillness.

Simon's housemother reported that Simon's speech continued to increase and that he would often give a running commentary on everything that was going on. However, he still referred to himself in the third person, as 'Simon'. His teacher noted that Simon went willingly to healing sessions and returned calmly from them. However, there were various changes to the usual school timetable towards the end of November and during December, and Simon, who depended for his security on set and predictable routines, reacted badly to this. This showed in some aggressive and violent behaviours towards others.

The Christmas holidays at home were quite difficult and Simon was put on medication to help reduce the likelihood of aggressive behaviours, probably due to anxiety and insecurity. When he returned to school in the New Year Simon appeared much more passive and there had been some reduction in his anxious behaviours. We managed five healing sessions but he missed two others owing to him coming down with a fluey illness in January 2006. Simon was co-operative and receptive to the healing, and he was less restless than before.

The last session was in the first week of February.

Session 44 – 6 February 2006

Simon came across quickly with E. (a helper) after morning assembly and going through the timetable in the classroom.

He sat straight down on the stool when he came in. He got up once, early on in the session and went towards the table but he did not touch anything, and he sat down straightaway again at my request. I experienced this as a peaceful, calm, session. There were no impulsive movements from Simon and no pressing on my hands with his. He co-operated willingly. My hand positions were – shoulders, head, along spine, heart, I tried 'top and tail' but he moved my hand, and back to shoulders. As before, I did the healing standing behind Simon and just going slightly to his side for the heart position. I don't have eye-to-eye contact with Simon.

He was certainly not restless, in any sense of the word, so I would say this was a good session with Simon being receptive. At the end he was still sat on the stool. I told him that we would finish and that he had 'done well' and that he would now go back to his teacher. I said 'goodbye' to him twice but he didn't reply.

The week's half-term, at home, actually went well, and Simon's aggression was minimal. Unfortunately, however, when he returned to school his behaviour was, for whatever reason, very insecure, obsessional and restless, and he was suddenly no longer 'passive' as he had been before, although the medication had not been stopped. Unfortunately, the school felt no longer able to meet Simon's complex needs and his increasingly challenging and risky behaviours. He was strong, had grown quickly and as a 14-year-old had, so to speak, plunged rapidly into puberty. I hope the healing sessions had helped to give Simon some greater measure of inner security and peacefulness than might otherwise have been the case, and had also contributed to the remarkable progress which he had achieved in his first year at the school.

Larry, diagnosed with Lowe's Syndrome and Asperger's type of autism

Larry was diagnosed by the age of six with a rare disease called Lowe's Syndrome. The oculocerebrorenal syndrome of Lowe (OCRL) is, I understand, an X-linked disorder involving several organ systems, including the eyes, nervous system and kidneys. Affected boys suffer numerous medical problems, and their families face a daunting burden. As a baby Larry had been floppy; had glaucoma and cataracts and had failed to thrive. He also had many chest infections during his first two years of life.

Larry had his first Grand Mal epileptic seizure when around 12 years of age. He had also been described as having an Asperger's type of autism and he had lots of obsessions and anxieties. At times he was bad tempered and aggressive to others. Fortunately, Larry had developed good speech.

Of course whatever medical diagnosis and prognosis a child receives, it is always the meeting with the child as a unique individual which forms the heart and core of curative education. To do everything possible to alleviate the given condition, however pervasive and profound it may be, is the impulse and aim of this curative work and also of course of my aim as a 'spiritual healer'.

I began to take Larry for healing sessions in May 2002 in the summer term, when he was already 17 years old. This was the first of a total of 50 sessions.

Session 1 – 8 May 2002

Larry was well aware of what he was coming to – to 'healing'. He does have problems with both knees, which can be painful (he said they were so). I therefore spent quite a bit of time giving healing for the knees. He tells me his eyes are OK.

I believe his condition, his syndrome, affects the kidneys, so perhaps the lower back area needs attention. Larry liked listening to the taped music, but I'll have to take care this doesn't become too engrossing for him as he has a particular interest in such 'machinery'.

Session 2 – 15 May 2002

Larry was quite restless at the start of the session, moving his hands, head, etc. But once the healing started he became very still and peaceful.

He told me, when I enquired, that his knees have not been aching so much but that his feet ached. He wears very thick-soled, supportive shoes.

He relaxed and liked the session.

His teacher tells me that Larry is physically in a very robust and well condition.

Session 3 – 22 May 2002

Larry is totally co-operative and receptive to healing. He told me he was feeling 'perfect'! He made no mention of any aches or pains in his knees or ankles. During healing I experienced a lot of heat over his knees.

He is interested in the music – classical or pop! I'm glad to give him some healing.

Session 4 – 29 May 2002

Larry was receptive and co-operative.

I asked him how he was and also if he had any aches with his knees or ankles – he said he didn't. I gave him a thorough healing, also over his eyes.

I noticed he had just the end of a wart (probably) on his left hand. I think he had one or two warts a couple of weeks ago.

The summer half-term, just a week, came and went. His housemother told me that Larry is 'in very good health', and that he had a good half-term at home – he's 'perfect'!

We continued where we had left off, and Larry also continued to be very receptive.

Session 7 – 26 June 2002

Larry is very willing to come and clearly he likes the session. He seems to be walking well. He does not complain about any aches in his legs. There is more warmth over his right knee than his left.

The session is peaceful, and he doesn't speak unless I ask him something.

Session 8 – 3 July 2002

Larry wasn't down for the session. Had a sprained ankle. So I went to his house and gave him healing specifically for the ankle. He seemed well and in good spirits.

Session 9 – 10 July 2002

His ankle is better to the extent that he walks on it, but obviously it still aches. I gave him healing for it today in the session. He said 'thank you', out of his own initiative.

For the summer term 2002, from May to July, Larry's housemother reported that he had been getting on very well, with improved mobility and no sign of epilepsy. He had been rather more obsessive in the last two or three weeks of term with words getting 'stuck', not only when reading but also in conversation. Apart from that he was in a good state and was physically more robust and stable.

We had no further sessions until the start of the new school year in September.

Session 10 – 4 September 2002
Larry came for healing today. He has a sore right knee and had obvious difficulties in walking. So I hope this will improve soon.

His housemother told me today that Larry had been very well over the holidays and that his sore knee was acquired in the swimming pool this week! Probably twisted or strained it somehow.

Session 11 – 11 September 2002
So Larry was 'perfect' today. He's walking normally again. I gave him a 'general' healing plus healing on knees, ankles, feet, eyes and kidneys.

Session 12 – 18 September 2002
Larry walks well pushing his wheelchair in front of him. No further problem with his knee. He looks to me to be in good physical shape.

Session 13 – 25 September 2002
Larry says he feels 'perfect'. Lately I've been impressed to see him walking and pushing his wheelchair in front of him. Seems able on his feet. Most warmth over the right knee. I'm aware of his kidney problems.

We continued until the two-week autumn half-term break, and then resumed in November.

Session 16 – 6 November 2002

I asked Larry how he was. He said, as usual, that he was 'perfect'. He said he used to have headaches, but now has less. His knees were not aching, however, he was making throaty noises quite often. He said he had a dry throat (not a sore one), and that he'd had some medicine during half-term – echinacea and paracetamol. Anyway he seems very well.

Session 18 – 20 November 2002

Larry seems to be, *is*, in very good physical shape. Walks well.

Apparently in school he's very 'with it', asks sensible questions and thinks about things. Strong voice.

Session 19 – 27 November 2002

I thought Larry was unwell and would not come to the healing session in Chalice. Therefore I went to see him in his house at rest hour after lunch to give him healing. This I did. He complained of some pain in his right knee *during* the healing! This was not my hope! I did spend most time on his feet, as he was in bed. Well, wait and see what happens.

As it was, he did get up and go to school in the afternoon. Sometimes, in my experience, a painful condition is temporarily 'localised' as part of the healing process.

Session 21 – 11 December 2002

Larry was calm and peaceful, not restless, in the healing today.

He does have a problem with getting sentences out in completion. He gets half or more of the way through, then has to go back and start again until he can finally get out all that he wants to say.

For the autumn term I received two brief reports from Larry's house-mother, before, and also after the half-term. For the first half of the term she said that he had been very well physically and far more mobile and active. Emotionally he was still very obsessive and repetitive in his speech but, all in all, very good. For the second half of the term she reported that Larry had been getting on very well but was rather excitable with all the special pre-Christmas events. However, his reading was a big problem because he got stuck over words – endlessly repeating them until he gets it right – sometimes for up to an hour. Physically he was, again, much more active. Apparently he'd had an excellent holiday.

Then the new year came.

Session 22 – 20 January 2003

Larry was waiting for me after his painting lesson. He sat well on the stool, without any back support. He said he was well and did not complain of any aches or pains, and I decided not to ask him specifically about this.

He co-operates well. I am aware of his various conditions – kidney problems, epilepsy, arthritis.

At the end of the session he got up quickly and was ready to be off!

Session 30 – 24 March 2003

Larry seems well. Didn't complain about his feet hurting this week – I asked him specifically about this.

I took his shoes off today and asked him to walk. His feet are very distorted in that he walks on tiptoe with his heels off the ground. (He wears built-up, supportive, shoes.) Anyway, seems well enough.

In the first week of April he had a cold and cough.

Session 32 – 14 April 2003

Unfortunately Larry is not in a good state at present. Rather withdrawn again. In the healing session he didn't speak, apart from a little in a very quiet voice. I hope he'll pick up again soon.

The Easter break came. Larry's teacher had given me a report for the spring term 2003 which said that Larry had generally been getting on excellently, and that 'in terms of physical health and flexibility he had never been better'. He rarely used his wheelchair and joined in with almost all movement activities. His physical stamina had increased. Larry's housemother confirmed that his general mobility had improved even more, and that he was getting on generally very well apart from increased obsessiveness when reading.

However, unfortunately Larry was not well enough to return to school during the first half of the summer term, having gone into a withdrawn state, and I did not see him for healing until June.

Session 33 – 16 June 2003

I saw Larry for healing today, but he's still not talking.

At the start of the session he was very restless – moving his hands a lot and also his upper body. In the session he became much more peaceful and still.

He had come willingly from his house with me to Chalice for the session.

Session 34 – 17 June 2003

Saw Larry again today. He was in his bed with the curtains closed but he then got up and came willingly with me to Chalice.

He was less restless and agitated than he was yesterday. He accepted the healing. Still not speaking audibly, but we must be patient.

Session 36 – 19 June 2003

Today Larry came at 3.30pm. Relaxed and still in the session. He also made physical contact with me, putting his hand to my hand and to the area, perhaps, where he needs it.

Afterwards I took him through the walled garden and asked him some questions. He answered, *not* in a whisper but in a quiet and clear voice. Good progress.

Unfortunately a week later he'd stopped speaking again and, before I saw him for his last session that summer term, he had two big tempers and had also shown some aggression.

Session 42 – 4 July 2003

I saw Larry again this afternoon. I went to his house. He was in his room listening to his radio. I said we could go to Chalice for healing and, eventually, after five or ten minutes perhaps, he switched off his radio and came.

A good, co-operative session. However, he's not speaking. I tried to elicit a word or two from him going to and returning from Chalice, but to no avail. He's going home this weekend and will have tests, I believe.

The summer holidays passed and the new school year began, but Larry had not returned to school. He was still not in a healthy state due to his epilepsy. Apparently he did have a couple of periods in the holidays when he came back to normal consciousness, but then slipped out again.

His parents are exhausted. There has been aggression from Larry. Drugs are increased. He's not completely mute, but restless. However, he did return to us in September.

Session 44 – 11 September 2003

Resumed healing with Larry. He's been back at school two or three days and seems in good shape. Talking again; about cord pulls on lights – repeatedly! – but *much more his old self*. He was co-operative and receptive in the session.

Larry continued to be in good voice through the autumn term though he only went part-time to school, as he needed space to himself. Sometimes he was restless and fidgety at the start of a healing session, but then settled down more peacefully.

Session 48 – 13 November 2003

He was not in school this afternoon, so I went to see him in his room. I asked him if he wanted some healing and he said that he did. He got out of bed and sat in his chair. His feet were cold. Larry was co-operative and not as restless as he was last week.

On Tuesday this week he took part in the short St Martin's play and spoke a sentence or two. By the end of November his housemother remarked that Larry was doing well – something of a miracle! In early December he went home for the weekend. He had his eighteenth birthday. But he then had some sickness and diarrhoea and, due to dehydration, was in hospital. When he returned we had our final session.

Session 50 – 11 December 2003

Saw Larry for the last session today. He's leaving the school this term to take up a 52-week placement.

He seems well again – speaking well – though rather stuck (as usual) on his particular interests.

Larry had always been receptive in the sessions and I believe he had enjoyed the healing and felt better for it. In fact, being a verbally able and articulate young man, he had said as much to his parents.

Larry had complex needs and, as with Simon before, there were quite long periods of very clear and positive progress and also times of definite setbacks and increased difficulties. It is, however, impressive to see how healing can create an 'oasis' of stillness and peace for such children who are so often restless and disturbed in body and mind.

Susan, diagnosed with meningo encephalitis brain damage and also within the autistic spectrum

Susan's early development appeared to be progressing well, even quite forward in some respects, until she had scarlet fever and a high persistent temperature when aged two and a half years. Thereafter, special needs and learning difficulties began to be noticed.

Medically, an initial diagnosis of post meningo encephalitis brain damage with emotional instability and signs of withdrawing was made. She was also described as functioning within the Autistic Spectrum, having a severe speech and language communication disorder, and Attention Deficit Hyperactivity Disorder (ADHD).

Susan was 16 years old when I began to take her for healing sessions. She had good, in fact very clear, speech but very poor fine motor control and co-ordination. She was easily distracted and lacked concentration, but was observant, sociable, and aware of and friendly towards others. Susan was generally cheerful but could also, sometimes, appear rather withdrawn and distant. She was emotionally very sensitive and reactive, and also vulnerable because of her lack of age-appropriate behaviours. She had a very likeable and 'sunny' personality, and she needed a warm and supportive approach from others in order to feel happy and secure.

Session 1 – 16 May 2002

Susan was receptive to healing. Sits quietly, no sound. As Susan's fingers were restless, I placed her hands on her legs to help her come to stillness. She was co-operative with this. Her back and neck were rather bent forwards – round shouldered.

When Susan walks she has lots of involuntary twisty movements of her arms and hands.

Session 2 – 23 May 2002

Susan is co-operative with healing. Sits quietly, no sound. Some restlessness – fiddling with fingers for example, and movement of head if I place my hands there. But a positive session. Strong warmth, e.g. over abdomen area.

She is very movement disturbed and very unable with fine motor skills.

Session 3 – 30 May 2002

Susan sits quietly on the chair for healing. She has severe motor control problems with regard to her arms and hands. Also problems to be attentive. There's a curvature of her spine; and she has bladder control problems at night. Her fingers were cool. She does not object to physical touch and is co-operative.

Then later, following the one-week summer half-term.

Session 5 – 4 July 2002

Susan was still, quiet and peaceful today. She co-operated well.

Her hands are cold and her fingertips almost look bluish. Clearly her own warmth does not penetrate through into her lower arms and hands.

Her shoulders were warm but from the elbows down she is cool – in fact her elbows felt quite cold.

It is striking that her lower arms and hands are so unpenetrated by her ego, and her hands and fingers engage in lots of twisty, involuntary movements (athetoid spasticity I presume?).

Session 6 – 11 July 2002

Took Susan for healing this morning. Again her arms are cold from elbow to fingertips. I tried to help warm them through with the healing.

Susan is amenable to hands-on healing. Yesterday at supper-time her carer noticed that Susan had interlinked the fingers of her hands when putting her hands together. It was, presumably, unusual for Susan to do this and she also did this in the session today. After the session she more or less ran back to Cinnabar (the seniors building).

Though this act of crossing the fingers of her two hands may seem rather insignificant to the ordinary observer, to a curative educator it can be interpreted as an important step in bodily awareness and in 'centering' oneself, as opposed to being simply drawn out into the surroundings. A similar step is seen when in simple form-drawing exercises a child goes through a 'crossing point' instead of bypassing it, e.g. when making a figure eight with a continuous line, instead of constructing it with two circles.

Interestingly two days later, her carer told me that Susan herself had said to her before she went home for the weekend, that Bob had helped to make her hands warmer. So it sounded as if Susan *did* feel warmer!

In the new school year after the summer holidays, we resumed our weekly sessions in September.

Session 8 – 16 September 2002

I took Susan for healing in Chalice. She was co-operative and receptive. Her hands and elbows are not as cold as they have felt sometimes before.

Session 11 – 7 October 2002

Susan is quiet and co-operative. When I asked her to sit up straight so that I could place my hands on her lower back area, I was impressed how upright she could sit! Before we finished I asked her to practise crossing the fingers of her two hands when putting them together, which she did with some help from me.

We continued our healing sessions, after the two-week half-term break.

Session 14 – 18 November 2002

Cold fingertips. Susan has now learnt to cross her fingers well when putting her hands together. I encourage her when walking to keep her arms down, and not sticking out at the sides. I feel she needs to gain more body awareness, which goes together with a more centred self-awareness.

Susan co-operates in healing.

Session 16 – 2 December 2002

Her hands are not so cold today as they often are. I feel with Susan it's the becoming aware of her body and controlling it better that's needed. She's also in daily life so unfocused – not looking at what she's doing, for instance.

Usually at the end of a healing session I also asked Susan to practise simple curative co-ordination exercises, such as crossing her fingers (i.e. interlacing the fingers of her two hands); standing up and putting her feet together as far as she could whilst keeping her balance; and putting out her arms horizontally and vertically. Susan co-operated with these bodily exercises, as she also did with the actual healing.

Her housemother commented for the autumn term that Susan had, after half-term, been more sensible, was talkative and could fold her hands (fingers) correctly. There were, however, ongoing problems with nocturnal enuresis.

Healing sessions continued in the spring term.

Session 18 – 20 January 2003

Susan co-operated in the session. She sat on the stool, instead of a chair. It was obvious that her back is not straight. It looked almost as if she had something of a slight hunchback. I believe she has a sort of lateral curvature of the spine. I included this therefore in the healing, seeking correction. Apparently nocturnal enuresis is still a problem and I brought this to her awareness with the hope that we try to improve matters.

Session 20 – 10 February 2003

She was talkative going down to the session. Last Friday her carer remarked that Susan had walked down the stairs in the house unaided and unsupported. This was new, she said.

Susan was alert and co-operative today.

We continued after the spring half-term.

Session 22 – 3 March 2003

Susan was fine in the session. Still, quiet, receptive. Hands warm except for her fingertips. Her back is very obviously out of line; appears pushed to one side at the mid-back.

Session 27 – 7 April 2003

Susan tends to sit round-backed on the stool. However, when asked to, and with an effort, she can sit much more upright. Her hands were warm, but the ends of her fingers cold.

At the end of the session we practised getting her feet closer together when standing. This is improving, I would say.

For the spring term her housemother reported that Susan had been 'generally settled', and that she responded best with adults that she knew well and who had a warm and friendly approach to her, so that Susan also then felt emotionally secure. After the Easter break we continued weekly healing sessions.

Session 28 – 12 May 2003

Susan seemed somewhat sleepy (or relaxed!) in the session. When she is really asked to 'sit up straight' she can achieve this quite impressively. Her hands were cold to begin with (she'd been outside), but very warm by the end of the session.

Session 29 – 19 May 2003

Much more 'awake' in the healing than last week. She can sit up very straight when asked to. Seemingly no aches or pains in her legs/knees that she could tell me about. (Susan was rather prone to such problems.)

After healing I was impressed how much better she was at getting her feet parallel and more nearly together when standing. I think there are some real improvements in her body awareness. Also in keeping her arms down when walking.

Following the week's half-term, healing sessions continued.

Session 32 – 23 June 2003

Susan was co-operative, peaceful, receptive. Her lower legs feel coldish, not warm. She doesn't properly penetrate to the ends of her extremities, i.e. fingers and toes.

Last week she was dry at night two or three times.

Session 34 – 7 July 2003

I have the impression that Susan is more 'together' somehow.

After the long summer break of about seven weeks we were ready to continue in the new school year. Susan's mother told me that Susan had had quite a good holiday. They had gone to France. However, she said that Susan had been afraid to come down some stairs. The impression is that so much depends on her feeling emotionally secure and happy.

Session 35 – 8 September 2003

Susan was co-operative, still and quiet.

Her hands were warmed through; she used to have markedly cold fingertips. The main thing with Susan is to feel safe, reassured and secure.

Session 36 – 13 September 2003

Susan is more able, with reminding, to sit upright and not to let herself slump forward. In the recent Review Meeting it was noted that Susan has made progress in self- and body awareness, being more 'centred' and more confident and with more age-appropriate behaviours.

After the two-week autumn half-term holidays.

Session 38 – 3 November 2003

I took Susan at the end of the morning. She was co-operative and receptive. I was impressed to see how upright she was standing after the healing. I almost thought she had grown! Generally she is less 'collapsible' and slumped over than she used to be.

Session 43 – 8 December 2003

Susan was co-operative. Clapping her hands a little. Her teacher told me that he'd noticed Susan seemed lopsided and unbalanced earlier in the morning. I told him that Susan's mother had informed us that Susan has a phobia about coming down the stairs at home.

Susan now has eurythmy therapy as well as healing. Could she be becoming more 'centred' and also more self-conscious, which might even make some tasks more difficult for her?

A few days later I noticed that Susan had now also become afraid of descending the stairs in her house at school. Anyway Christmas and the holidays were fast approaching, and after that a new year to continue to support her in her development.

Session 44 – 12 January 2004

Susan came for healing today.

I understand that during the Christmas holidays it was not easy at home. She didn't want to come down the stairs, nor go to the loo. She saw a cranial osteopath who said she was 'tensed up'.

In healing Susan was less dreamy and vacant than she used to be. My impression is that she is more 'centred' and less passive.

At the end of the session when I asked her to stand up and put her feet together, she did this better than I've seen her do it before. She put the left foot across to join the other and it didn't move back again – but stayed! I was very impressed – a definite change from how she used to do it.

I asked Susan if she was happy to continue with weekly healing and she said 'yes' (though not with great enthusiasm!).

Session 45 – 19 January 2004

I do think Susan is more 'with it' somehow than she used to be. Physically more able to hold herself upright. Certainly she can put her feet better together – or at least closer together than she could last term.

We continued through the spring term, and again after the Easter break in May 2004.

Session 50 – 3 May 2004

I saw Susan today. She seemed relaxed and amenable to healing. Was co-operative throughout.

The ends of her fingers were rather cool. She sat rather hunched over at the neck, and I encouraged her to try to sit up straight.

The main aim of healing, as I see it, is to help Susan get better into herself (into her body), to become more 'centred' and more penetrated through by her ego and by warmth.

Session 54 – 21 June 2004

Susan was co-operative, as usual. Cool fingers. Still has her spine defect. Sat still and quietly. Unfortunately there is still nocturnal enuresis, but no problem with stairs anymore, not at school nor at home.

Susan left the school that year as she was 18 years old. I had the impression that healing may well have helped her, and certainly it had created a peaceful, quiet space, again and again. Susan had gained better body awareness over the year, as also confirmed by her parents' observations. She was more confident, could verbalise better what she wanted to say and was able to make real choices. Furthermore, and importantly, if there was a problem Susan could say what the matter was without simply reacting emotionally as she used to.

At her eighteenth birthday party attended by guests and family it was very clear what a popular, sociable and confident young lady Susan was. She was indeed the belle of the ball!

Harry, diagnosed with hypoxic brain damage and epilepsy

Harry was born, nearly three weeks later than expected, by emergency Caesarean Section. The baby was in some distress and put on a ventilator. He had neonatal convulsions and renal failure. His developmental milestones were delayed and, at age eight, he had the first of his habitual epileptic seizures.

Medically Harry was diagnosed as having suffered hypoxic brain damage, and he had a long-standing problem with constipation. He had severe learning difficulties, poor concentration, a degree of clumsiness and was small-headed. Epilepsy was a main problem and he was, of course, on anticonvulsant medication but his seizures were not sufficiently controlled by this treatment.

Harry was a good-looking 17-year-old young man, tall, lean and long-limbed, who appeared rather shy and reticent when I first took him for healing sessions in May 2002.

Session 1 – 13 May 2002

Harry came with me to Chalice. I told him what I would do and he seemed OK with this. I gave him a shorter healing session today than planned for, so that he would feel reassured about it.

Harry sat with his head bowed forward, eyes closed. He seemed relaxed though I observed slight nervous movements in his fingers, but nothing to be concerned about.

He is a man of few words it seems. I did ask him some questions to try to engage him in conversation, when going to and from Chalice. He answers only briefly.

I felt this first session was fine.

Session 2 – 20 May 2002

He seemed OK to come with me. Harry sits bent forward a bit. Peaceful, still, receptive. I feel it would be good to work on his middle, heart area.

Afterwards he went back alone to Cinnabar. He must have gone back quickly and arrived all right at woodwork. He's friendly, but quiet – not a great talker, it seems.

Session 3 – 27 May 2002

I felt Harry had warmed up more today in his social-communication aspect. He was more ready to answer any questions I asked him. There was more contact and communication.

Harry's hands were warm at the start of the session but his fingers were decidedly cool in comparison. By the end of the session, and already quite early on, his fingers were also warmed through. He seemed quite happy to be here. However, I note that there is a slight trembling in his arms and hands.

After the short summer half-term break we continued in June.

Session 4 – 10 June 2002

I fetched Harry from Cinnabar. He told me he had a new coat and that he'd spent half-term with his father.

In the healing session he was more 'restless' than he's been before. (Before half-term he had had his head tilted forward and was quiet and still.)

Today he was more curious and looking to see what I was doing. For example, when I passed my hands over his head and around him at the end (not touching), he tilted his head right back with wide-open eyes to look. On the other hand I didn't notice that slight trembling of his hands which I have seen before.

I asked Harry a couple of times if he felt something, anything, during the healing. Mostly he said 'no', though my left hand over his upper chest area he said was 'cold'. I also asked him if he liked coming to the session and he said he did. So Harry seems OK with this.

Apparently at a previous school he was showing very challenging behaviours. Here it seems he's settled and getting on well.

So as regards healing, perhaps it is a matter of bringing better *balance* to his energy field; helping his self-confidence and esteem; and alleviating any hidden anxieties, fears or insecurities.

Harry makes eye-to-eye contact with me, at times too prolonged!

His housemother told me that his week's half-term holiday went well.

Session 6 – 29 June 2002

Harry is certainly much more 'open', sociable and talkative with me now than he was when we started. In the session I asked him to keep his head up. He is more active and curious to see what I'm doing than he was to start with. However, he co-operates well.

Session 7 – 8 July 2002

I had about a 15-minute session with Harry. It's not easy for him to really *relax*, I think. He's quiet and co-operative, and he does appear to like the session from what he says when I ask him afterwards.

Talking with his housemother that evening, at the end of term, she said that Harry's parents were going to try to find a spiritual healer for him during the summer holidays. Obviously they felt that he'd benefited from this experience for his epilepsy.

She also reported that he had had a very good summer term, and that he was becoming more independent and gaining in confidence, and his bowel problems were not as marked as before. He was helpful, positive and social. However, the biggest significant change was that there had been no epileptic seizures since 28 May, whereas prior to this Harry was having three or four a month.

I was ready to take Harry for healing again in the new school year in September. Apparently he had had no seizures in the long summer holidays. However, he'd had one fit since being back at school that week. Apparently Harry had been having some Reiki healing in the holidays. He also started to have twice weekly eurythmy therapy this September at school.

Session 8 – 2 September 2002

I took Harry for healing today. He does find it difficult to just relax; he tends to fiddle with his fingers, etc. His posture is tending to curve over when he's sat, and when I put my hands on his head he lets his head go forwards and down. I asked him to try and sit more upright.

He is co-operative, but it would be good if he could relax more. Harry said, when I asked him, that he had gone for healing also in the holidays.

Session 11 – 25 September 2002

Harry finds it difficult to really sit still in the session. He moves his head. I feel that he's not entirely comfortable with me touching him. I wonder if he should just have a break from healing, and then see how he is regarding seizures?

Session 13 – 16 October 2002

I asked Harry today if he would like a break from healing after half-term. He said he would. I did this because he obviously finds it difficult to relax and sit still in healing, and anyway he now has individual eurythmy therapy.

Harry's housemother informed me that in September, unfortunately, epileptic seizures had started again, after quite a long break of about three months. Apart from this he was generally getting along fine in the autumn term. His biggest problems were lack of concentration and bowel awareness. For the second half of the autumn term she wrote that his confidence had increased and he was having hardly any fits. He had also had an 'excellent' two weeks half-term holiday.

I saw Harry again for healing in the summer term 2003 and found him to be co-operative, comfortable and more relaxed than before with the sessions. During the long summer holidays I heard that he had had a couple of bigger fits and also that constipation was a problem. In the new school year in September, we resumed healing. The sessions were quite short, 10 to 15 minutes each.

Session 20 – 25 September 2003

Harry came willingly for healing. He finds it difficult to just sit still and really relax. He looks up at me at times. However, he seems more settled now into the term. Basically willing and co-operative.

I continued with our sessions into October and November but could see that Harry still found it rather difficult to be at ease and simply receive the healing. His nineteenth birthday was soon to come.

Session 24 – 27 November 2003

Harry finds it difficult to just sit and receive. He's too self-conscious in a way. I ask him to sit up straight, otherwise he rather flops over.

At the end of today's session I asked him if he wants to continue to come to healing or would prefer not to. He said clearly that he prefers not, so I told him that after this term (just two more sessions), we would give it a break. I respected, of course, his wishes.

I had therefore my last sessions with Harry in December 2003.

In Summer 2004 it was reported that Harry was doing well. His concentration and independence had improved, and he had matured generally. He had on average one or two fits a month. Harry was said to be generally more confident, able to participate in conversations, was sensible and, importantly, to have a great sense of humour!

I had been happy to get to know him through our healing sessions which I hoped had contributed towards his positive progress and maturity.

Ben, diagnosed with a complex chromosome abnormality and global developmental delay

As the reader will appreciate, most of the pupils I was seeing for healing were already teenagers and adolescents. Ben, however, was still ten years old when I first saw him for spiritual healing sessions in the autumn term 2004.

Ben had a complex chromosome abnormality and global developmental delay. He also had a congenital anomaly of the kidneys, and a severe lymph oedema of the left leg. Although his learning difficulties were severe, the most outstanding features with Ben were his emotional and behavioural difficulties. He demanded a great deal of attention and his challenging behaviours had included screaming episodes, slapping people's faces, spitting and tearing up books. In the classroom his loud shouting could be very disruptive. Ben's speech and communication were very restricted and he had only a few words and phrases with which to convey his wishes and needs. He was described as being largely egocentric and not showing any real interest in interacting with his peers. On the other hand in certain situations Ben could also be a happy and friendly boy, though he needed a firm and consistent approach. On a one-to-one basis Ben could be very co-operative and willing to participate in activities.

Session 1 – 11 October 2004

I took Ben for the first time for healing today. He was probably a bit over-awed. Anyway this session went well. He sat on the stool and was still and quiet.

He has a very swollen lower left leg, with some pink protuberance on it also. So I spent time giving healing to this leg, which is much bigger than his right leg. The right one was warm, but the left leg (filled with fluid?) was cooler.

Ben co-operated well. When we were going back to his class he came out with some very loud noises, but then went quietly back into the classroom.

Session 2 – 14 October 2004

I took Ben for the second time this week and fetched him from the play-ground. He came willingly to Chalice. I helped take his coat off and he came in and sat very properly on the stool, his hands together.

Ben was 'well contained' in the session. He spoke a little but I deliberately did not strike up any conversation – keeping it peaceful and quiet, with the music as a background. I gave him general healing, but also specifically for his left swollen leg.

At the end of the session when I said it was time to go he didn't straight-away get up. In fact I had to take his hands to make it clear to him that it was time to go. He then went dashing to the treatment room, but I simply steered him to his coat and back out to the playground.

Session 3 – 21 October 2004

Ben co-operated well. After a time he did start to speak but it did not disturb the session. His left leg is still swollen, but I wondered if it was perhaps a little less than a week ago.

Today we had a visitor sitting in from the university, and Ben was aware of this.

The two-week autumn half-term intervened.

Session 4 – 8 November 2004

When I fetched Ben from the classroom late afternoon, he came quite enthu-siastically!

He was very talkative in the session and I had, repeatedly, to make it clear to him that he should rather sit quietly during the healing. He was more talk-ative than before half-term, though it's very difficult to understand what he's saying. However, for the first session back and after a day in school, it was all right.

His left leg is still very swollen, with this strange pink blob on it around the knee area.

Session 5 – 11 November 2004

The very first session I had with Ben, in October, he was very still and quiet, but the two sessions since half-term he's been rather talkative.

Today he was testing me a bit by, for example, moving the chair at the side of the stool and he had a very cheeky look on his face at times with bright, shiny, eyes.

I therefore took a very clear line with him, not allowing him to please himself but with a clear level of expectation. Given this, he managed well actually.

He strikes me as having a smallish head, and a very swollen, out-of-shape left leg, which I spent some time on. The leg is coolish to the touch and presumably filled with excess fluid. Maybe healing can get things flowing and moving there?

What is wrong with Ben? What could healing help to improve? How could he benefit?

Certainly in coming to peace and quiet. This would be important for him. Somehow he's too bright and 'sparky'.

Also to bring him into balance. He doesn't walk properly with his over-sized leg. He needs a sense for balance – also in his soul probably. When he speaks he's often loud and shouts. His front teeth stick out too far making clear articulation very difficult.

I continued to have twice weekly sessions with Ben. He co-operated well, even though he didn't manage to sit still and quietly throughout the entire length of each session. When he does speak outside of a session he is often very loud – it's almost as if it explodes out of him! However, I couldn't understand a word he said because of his very poor articulation. On the other hand he appeared to understand when he was spoken to.

I saw his teacher after one of the sessions and she said that Ben was peaceful after his healing session. Apparently he does have words and, occasionally, speaks sentences clearly but with the words all strung together. His swollen leg is supposed to be an incurable condition. I did find Ben to be an interesting and likeable boy, and at the end of sessions he remained sitting and I had to insist that it was time to go! He always needed very clear expectations about acceptable behaviour in the sessions but, given that, it went well and we continued into December.

Session 10 – 9 December 2004

I just ran across with him. He's not sat quietly on the stool waiting to start, but is noisy making little sounds like 'heh'. I have to ask him repeatedly to sit quietly. I think he does things to test and tease and to try to get a reaction. Anyway overall the session works with him.

He pulled up his trousers to show me his lower legs. There's no obvious change as yet in his 'water-leg'. He's pretty able on his feet considering this physical imbalance.

He does need clear expectations and directions, or he could be quite an imp!

After the Christmas holidays we made a good start in the New Year, in January 2005.

Session 11 – 20 January 2005

Quite a remarkable session for its quietness, stillness and co-operation.

Ben sat *still for 20 minutes*. I avoided making eye contact with him or speaking to him as, from past experience, I know this can encourage him to chatter and be more restless. It is best, I feel, to proceed clearly with the hands-on, while avoiding eye contact that can lead to him talking.

He needs, I believe, to come to peace and quiet. (He was talking rapidly on the way to Chalice, but I could not make out what he was saying.) I gave healing attention to his left swollen leg. It doesn't appear to have diminished in size since last term. He has this smooth, rounded and hard lump near the knee on that leg. He also has a white dressing (plaster) on this leg near the knee area; perhaps he has a scratch or soreness there?

Whereas his right, normal-sized leg, feels warm to the touch, his swollen leg is noticeably cooler. What is needed to remove this excess fluid in the left leg?

So overall a very good first session this New Year. However, when I had finished he was reluctant to get up and leave, and I had to take him by his hands – he then also made a few loud noises when he went out.

Session 12 – 24 January 2005

Ben was a bit more of his usual self today. Trying out to see how far he could go. I made my expectations clear and, with that, he complied pretty well.

He certainly has a very mischievous, cheeky streak. He was a bit talkative, but not much.

However, he didn't make loud noises after the session and I took him over to the schoolhouse – put his eurythmy shoes on him – and delivered him into his lesson.

Session 13 – 27 January 2005

Ben didn't talk at all during the session! He co-operated well, sitting quietly and still. I spent quite a lot of time on his swollen left leg. I can't see any noticeable changes as yet, but perhaps over the weeks the swelling will reduce?

I continue to deliberately keep a quiet and clear line with Ben in order that he behaves himself, as he certainly can be testing and cheeky if he has half the chance!

We continued into February until half-term and resumed again after the week's holiday. He remained co-operative, and I kept my clear expectations towards him.

Session 19 – 3 March 2005

Ben was very quiet, still and co-operative in this session. I gave him the 'general' healing first (from head, to spine, to chest), before going to his left leg specifically.

I thought the leg had a tiny bit more shape and was not quite so swollen. He did not have a dressing over the 'wound' near his knee. The skin had formed into a sort of blister – very reddish – but was contained with no obvious seeping of fluid.

The left leg was warmer than previously, but decidedly cool around the ankle area. Could this be where the 'blockage' is situated? Well, we'll see how it looks next week. A good, positive, session.

Session 21 – 10 March 2005

I've just fetched Ben from class – he came willingly – and is now sat quietly on the stool waiting.

He sat quietly and still throughout the session. Why doesn't the warmth penetrate through his left leg? Is the ego not able to take charge of this and control the fluid (etheric), watery element? That's how it seems. So to help his ego organisation to get into that left leg would be the task. For this it needs the warmth organism to work there also.

I took him back to class after. He was well behaved.

Session 22 – 14 March 2005

A good healing session with him. He was very quiet, still and co-operative.

I concentrated most of the time on his left leg (which his housemother believes is less swollen than it used to be).

Ben went home towards the end of March to have an operation on his left leg, I believe to remove the pink protuberance. After the Easter holidays we had a further four sessions in the summer term, in May.

Session 25 – 9 May 2005

Ben was 'playing up' in the playground, before he came to healing. His teacher had to call him down – actually fetch him down – from the climbing frame.

However, in the healing he was co-operative and quiet. I worked again on his left leg, which may have a bit more shape to it now.

Session 26 – 12 May 2005

He had made a lot of fuss, with screaming, before he came to healing.

However, once again in the session he was perfectly all right, quiet and co-operative. I didn't speak to him at all (in order that he should remain calm), and I worked again on his swollen leg.

In the summer term, in July, his annual review meeting took place and his parents said they were pleased with Ben's progress over the year. He had gradually changed and become generally calmer. However, both the school and house reports pointed out that about two weeks after the Easter holidays he had become very difficult in his behaviours, often refusing to co-operate, screaming very loudly and being provocative, though by that time I was no longer taking him for healing sessions. Interestingly, he had gone through a similarly difficult, uncooperative phase of behaviour the previous year also after the Easter holidays so, in this respect, it was nothing new. Ben's behaviour did, apparently, go in phases of better or worse.

Still it had often been striking to see just how quiet and contained Ben had been in our healing sessions even when, sometimes, he had been loud and 'out of himself' before he came. Even though the twice weekly sessions were but a very small part of Ben's school week, nonetheless their combined effect may well have contributed to his good progress and generally calmer presentation.

After the summer holidays 2005 Ben made a planned transfer to a different Camphill School in order to be nearer his home, so further healing sessions were unfortunately not possible.

Brenda, diagnosed with Autistic Spectrum Disorder

Brenda was very delayed in her development of speech and only spoke her first words at around seven years of age. At two years she was diagnosed as being on the Autistic Spectrum. However, it was a profound inability in language and particularly in the receptive understanding of speech, which seemed to be at the core of her disabilities. Developmentally her autistic features were probably of a secondary nature in relation to this primary language problem. As she grew up Brenda depended on predictable routines in order to make sense of the world around her. She did show at times some rather obsessive activities, such as shredding leaves for hours. However, Brenda was generally friendly and 'sociable' to others and willing to co-operate, though if she didn't get what she wanted when she wanted it, difficult behaviours could arise. She was a pretty, round-faced and largish-headed young lady when I first took her for healing sessions in May 2002. She was then 11 years old and, although she could repeat words in copying what others said (echolalia), her actual comprehension of language was still very limited and she often relied on visual cues.

Session 1 – 16 May 2002
Brenda came with me to Chalice and she offered me her hand to take.

She was co-operative in the healing and she looked at me a lot with her big blue eyes. Brenda repeated any words or sounds I said. She is willing to communicate and, after healing, I named some objects in the room for her to name also – chair, table, curtains, tape recorder.

Session 2 – 23 May 2002

Co-operative. Looks at me directly. When my hands were over her throat area she made some sounds spontaneously. Brenda is stocky, robust, well-built, active. I named and touched tables, chairs, etc. with her, trying to stimulate some concepts.

Session 3 – 30 May 2002

I took Brenda today for 15 to 20 minutes, which is enough for her.

She sits peacefully on the chair and sometimes looks at me with her big, wide-open eyes. No trouble with eye-to-eye contact!

I don't know what healing can do for her. Her problem is, I'm sure, a receptive aphasia, a lack of conceptual understanding through the word. Maybe healing can help alleviate any inner tension, frustration, that builds up in her?

Anyway, she is fully co-operative.

However, I was not sure just how relevant healing sessions were for Brenda and, after these first sessions in the summer term, I did not take Brenda for healing again until the autumn term 2002, in November.

Session 4 – 6 November 2002

I thought it might be good to try again with Brenda, so I took her today for about 15 minutes. She sat still and was peaceful. A positive session.

I think it is worth seeing Brenda once a week to see if the healing helps her in some way. For example, to sleep easier; help word understanding; reduce obsessional behaviours.

Session 6 – 20 November 2002

She came willingly, taking my hand – her initiative. Sits quietly in healing. I think she's sleeping better in the house, getting off to sleep a bit quicker and easier.

Session 8 – 11 December 2002

Brenda comes quite happily. Sits still and is OK with hands-on. Peaceful.

Her housemother reported that for the second half of the autumn term Brenda was well settled in the house-life and used single words spontaneously. She was also quite relaxed. Brenda was dependent on established relationships with known adults. She had made good progress with practical tasks, such as washing the floor, and she was more adventurous with food and less 'stuck' on a particular diet.

After the Christmas holidays we resumed, weekly, in the spring term.

Session 9 – 27 January 2003

Co-operates well. Comes willingly. Holds my hand. Does not object to hands-on. Indeed *she* pressed my hands today, exerting more pressure.

Session 10 – 3 February 2003

Receptive to the healing. Does not object to being touched. When I sit in a position where she can see me, she often makes prolonged eye contact.

After the healing I spent some time just naming her body parts, e.g. arms, legs, feet, nose, ears, head, etc. asking her to say *'my* feet', etc. As such Brenda has no concept, it seems, of personal pronouns as an experience and expression of *herself.*

Session 12 – 17 February 2003

Brenda seems perfectly happy to be in the healing session. She does not object to being touched – in fact I have to take care that *she* does not press my hands to her too firmly!

Brenda has a major understanding, communication problem. She usually only goes to sleep late in the evening.

We continued in the same vein after the one-week spring half-term.

Session 15 – 17 March 2003

She always seems cheerful and quite happy. Keeps in good, robust health, I believe.

Session 18 – 7 April 2003

Another positive session. As well as practising speaking, 'I' and 'you' at the end, I also named various objects in the room, including wall, floor, carpet, etc. I think Brenda does require a real expectation towards her to use words and language.

I received some brief written reports from Brenda's housemother and teacher for that spring term. Her housemother said that Brenda had been mostly settled, and co-operated generally well when given clear levels of expectation in regard to conduct and skills. However, it was important that she was helped to *understand* what was asked of her. Brenda had been going to sleep earlier at night and she displayed fewer repetitive 'mannerisms'.

Her teacher commented that Brenda's communication was better and that she was communicating her 'wishes and needs more and more'.

In the summer term we continued weekly and I also carried out practising the correct usage of speech with her directly after the hands-on healing. Brenda was always co-operative, receptive and willing.

Both her housemother and teacher confirmed that Brenda was well settled most of the time and 'generally fine', though her teacher added that she was 'still very much in her own world'. Neither of them had noticed any particular changes with Brenda in the summer term.

The summer holidays arrived and, at home, I believe that Brenda's parents were pleased with her progress and her *more spontaneous use of speech*. In the new school year I resumed our healing sessions and speech exercises.

Session 26 – 8 September 2003

With Brenda I have to give her clear limits regarding physical contact. She co-operates well. At the end, when we practised naming and pointing to body parts she remembered this well and said, 'my arms' and so on.

She needs to learn simple phrases, as well as the names of objects.

Session 34 – 8 December 2003

Brenda was fine as usual. After the healing I spent a little time with her in speaking about *the position* of a box of tissues, e.g. put the box *on* the table, etc. I did this to encourage her use and understanding of language. She at first appeared not to understand at all, but, with a few tries, she was 'getting it' a little.

This speech work was of course an addition to the healing *per se*, but was, I felt, very important for Brenda and therefore justified within the time we had for our sessions. We continued in the New Year.

Session 35 – 12 January 2004

Brenda is quiet, co-operative and receptive as usual.

After the healing I spent a bit of time speaking with her, giving her instructions such as: to put my watch *on* the table, chair, stool, etc. or *by* the tape recorder, window, etc. in order to practise her understanding of prepositions. She did this well, actually!

She seemed to improve with these exercises as we continued through the spring term.

After the Easter break the summer term started.

Session 40 – 3 May 2004

Brenda was a little upset when she came across to Chalice. I don't know why. Perhaps she had had to leave some task that she liked doing in class?

Anyway she was co-operative in the session and was quite happy by the end of it. She can sit up very upright when asked to and often does this anyway of her own initiative. I did not do any communication exercises after the healing today.

She looked very pale today.

Session 41 – 17 May 2004

Brenda is co-operative. Sits upright.

Afterwards I did some word understanding with her. For example, asking her to put the tissue box in various places. She actually understood and did what was meant better than previously, even putting the box on her head or on her shoes upon request!

Session 42 – 31 May 2004

Just a short session today before she has eurythmy therapy. Brenda co-operates well and appears comfortable with the healing.

We had a total of 43 healing sessions. I found it difficult to judge how healing had been of benefit to her, but she certainly appeared to like and appreciate our sessions. She was now 13 years old and her housemother reported that Brenda had appeared to become more self-aware in the course of the year, and that she was less distant and oblivious than she used to be. She had made progress in her eurythmy therapy sessions, which she had from January to July 2004, becoming 'more present' and 'more flexible and inwardly more active and engaged'. She had also, recently, had the benefit of some weekly music therapy.

Therefore it is important to appreciate, as I have mentioned before, that Brenda, like other pupils, had received numerous inputs to try to help alleviate her learning disabilities and to develop her potentials. This included the speech work which I did with her after the healing.

CHAPTER 6

Healing Sessions III

Peter, diagnosed with global developmental delay in language, with fine and gross motor problems and hypotonia

Seemingly Peter's early development was within normal limits until around 18 months, when he was walking on the sides of his feet and needed special boots. By two and a half years there was considerable speech delay, though investigations did not reveal any particular syndrome.

He showed a global developmental delay in language with fine and gross motor problems, and was regarded as having severe learning difficulties. He also had hypotonia, wore splints to support his lower legs and required physiotherapy supervision. A major problem in day-to-day living was Peter's challenging behaviours at home. He could be stubborn and aggressive, have lengthy tantrums and it was becoming more difficult to control him as he became older and bigger. Generally his sleep was erratic and he was a very early riser.

I began weekly healing sessions with Peter when he was 15 years old and, in keeping with his parents' wishes, he was always accompanied by his housemother who knew him very well.

Session 1 – 6 September 2004
Peter sat as 'good as gold' on the stool. Quiet and still and receptive.

He wears splints on both legs. He's subject to tremors but I didn't see anything of these today, except perhaps a very slight movement of the head. In fact he seemed remarkably composed, self-contained and 'with it'!

His hands were warm – not cold.

Peter is not able, it seems, to stand up with his feet really together, one of his knees sticks out rather – the left one I think.

His housemother was present throughout the session.

Session 2 – 13 September 2004

T. (his housemother) was again present. Peter is perfect in the session. Sits up straight, is still and quiet. Totally co-operative. His hands were a little cool to begin, though his wrists were warm, but in the session his hands became warmed through.

T. says he sleeps OK at present. His speech articulation has also improved over time. I find Peter very receptive to healing.

Session 3 – 20 September 2004

Peter's hands were coldish to begin, but warm by the end of the session. T. says he sleeps OK. His parents were pleased with his progress, in a recent review meeting.

Session 4 – 27 September 2004

The model pupil! Sits upright, quiet, totally co-operative, and I feel he's very receptive. T. thinks he's sleeping OK. I asked her to look out for any improvements in leg tonus and body tremors.

Peter stands very upright.

Session 5 – 11 October 2004

Peter seemed a bit tired today. His hands were warm and clammy (probably got a bit warmer in the session). Sits still and is peaceful. I feel a lot of 'energy' around Peter somehow. Asked T. if she'd noticed any change in muscle tone in his legs. She remarked that he had less tremor. Sleep has not been good lately. (Last Monday I couldn't take Peter for healing.) See how sleep goes this week.

Peter is very upright, a special person.

We continued again after the two-week autumn half-term.

Session 6 – 15 November 2004

Peter did come today with T. (Couldn't give him healing last week as T. wasn't available to accompany him.) He is very co-operative and receptive to healing. He sits still and is quiet.

It seems he sleeps reasonably, though not so well at weekends, according to T.

Muscle tonus in his legs? T. wasn't sure. His hands warmed up in the session.

Session 8 – 29 November 2004

He came with T. again.

Peter's hands are soft and look unformed – unpenetrated. He sits quietly and still. T. says the muscle tone in his legs is still low. Sleeping was better it seems this past week.

Peter wants to communicate, but his speech is very inarticulate.

Christmas came, and after the holidays we continued in the New Year, 2005.

Session 9 – 24 January 2005

Peter came with T. today. Apparently he has a cold.

Peter is very receptive to healing – lots of warmth. He sits quietly and still. Totally co-operative. His hands were cool to start but very warm by the end. Hope to see improvement in his muscle tone in his lower legs. Twenty-minute session.

Session 10 – 7 February 2005

I didn't see Peter last week as I was away. T. said today that Peter has been shouting in the house and not in a very good mood. I asked him not to shout in the house.

He absorbs healing like a sponge. His hands especially warm up a lot, from being cool to begin with.

I asked him what he felt when I had my hands on his legs – he said it felt 'hot'. (T. translated this for me, as it's not easy to understand Peter with his poor articulation.)

Apparently he's sleeping all right.

We observed, again and again, how markedly Peter's normally cool hands warmed up in the healing sessions. This was an impressive, clearly observable, physical change, which the healing brought about with him.

After the spring half-term the three of us resumed our sessions.

Session 11 – 21 February 2005

Peter's parents were pleased with him during half-term. He's sleeping well.

He has a bit of a cold at present. His speech is difficult to understand, though Peter knows what *he* wants to say. His upper front teeth are too far forward – he can't put his lips together.

He's co-operative as ever.

Very flaccid, weak muscles in lower legs. Has a hereditary tremor also.

Session 12 – 7 March 2005

Peter's hands were cold to start with but warmed up *very strikingly* during the session. T. says his hands are always cold, except in healing!

He's practising to speak more clearly and to close his mouth better. He's very receptive to healing.

Session 13 – 14 March 2005

Had healing with Peter, again with T. present.

It is impressive just how hot Peter's normally cool hands become in the healing session. Today I also worked on his feet by taking off his shoes and callipers, and putting my hands on his rather cool feet. They also warmed up then.

Peter is very receptive to healing, and T. said he appears to enjoy the sessions. His annual review's coming up this Friday.

After the Easter holidays we had just two sessions in the summer term.

Session 14 – 25 April 2005

Saw Peter today with T. His hands were decidedly cool to begin with, but in the session became *hot* (not just warm).

I also removed his shoes and splints to work on his feet. His feet were cool (not icy cold), but were somewhat warmer by end of session.

T. says his speech is improving well. In the session Peter nearly goes to sleep! He is ideal for healing because he's so relaxed and laid back!

It is probably true to say that the more relaxed and receptive a person is in a spiritual healing session, the more beneficial the healing can be for them. The healer needs also to relax in order that the energy can flow through him or her.

Session 15 – 9 May 2005

Saw Peter again. His hands, especially the fingertips, were cold. By the end of the session they were hot, and the skin colour had changed to reddish. (Would look good on video!) T. says he has very little strength in his hands. So I've recommended that he squeezes others' hands (in a handshake), to strengthen and become more aware of his own hands. Peter's parents are pleased with his progress.

Various reports for the year 2004–2005 attested to Peter's good progress. He had, it seems, become more 'awake' and 'self-aware', as well as improving in speech and independence skills. In fact T. wrote that he had 'changed tremendously during the past year', whilst his teacher commented on a 'general sense of quiet composure' with Peter. Another regular review meeting noted that 'Peter was benefiting from healing sessions with Bob' and heard, with surprise, that during these sessions Peter was 'quiet for 20 minutes' and that, at the end of the healing 'his hands were warm;' both these states were apparently very unusual for Peter.

I had the impression that, together with many other inputs towards meeting Peter's special needs, healing was also having a definite and positive contribution to make. Certainly the dramatic physical change of temperature in Peter's hands during healing was always impressive to perceive. We had just a total of 15 sessions as more were not possible at that time.

Dora, diagnosed with complex difficulties; reportedly William's Syndrome and autistic features

Dora was small at birth and therefore spent some time in an incubator. However, the main developmental milestones seemed to proceed normally, though with some delay in language. However, as she was growing up Dora was seen to have complex difficulties, particularly in the realm of social understanding and interrelationships. Reportedly William's Syndrome and autistic features were said to contribute to her complex profile, though the most outstanding condition was her very high levels of anxiety. She was certainly emotionally very sensitive and vulnerable, and Dora very much depended on the support and security which familiar others could provide for her. Without sufficient understanding from others of her anxieties and fears Dora could easily over-react, even at times rather aggressively. Her good potentials for learning and social development were much influenced by her existential feelings of insecurity and her emotional hypersensitivity. She could be said to have a rather classic 'hysteric constitution' in curative educational terms and to be not sufficiently contained within the boundary of her own skin.

I first took Dora for healing sessions in October 2002, when she was 13 years old. In total we were then to have some 69 healing sessions, of which it will of course be only possible here to give a certain limited selection.

Session 1 – 9 October 2002

Just 15 minutes or so. She was a bit giggly, but actually 'well-contained' and quiet and still for the most part.

Session 2 – 10 October 2002

As A. (another pupil) wasn't back, I took Dora again today. She was giggly a couple of times but, on the whole, well-contained, peaceful and still.

Session 3 – 16 October 2002

She was fine in the session. Little bit giggly, but no problem. Sits quietly, upright and is sensible. Dora is receptive to receiving healing.

Session 4 – 17 October 2002

Again a little giggly, but she pulled herself together well and sat quietly. My main wish is to help to 'contain her', to help her get more peaceful and centred in herself. She doesn't talk at all in the session!

There was a two-week autumn half-term.

Session 6 – 13 November 2002

Very out of herself and silly at lunchtime in the house and also at washing-up afterwards. However, in healing she was perfect, not a laugh or giggle. Sat perfectly still and quiet.

Session 8 – 20 November 2002

She seems to enjoy and look forward to the healing sessions. Sits quietly – peaceful. Restless with her fingers today, but co-operative. She needs help to draw in and 'contain' herself.

Dora continued to respond in a similar way in the sessions we had until the end of the autumn term. Dora's housemother reported for the autumn term that mostly, with keeping to a known routine and familiar adults, Dora was calm and felt secure. She still sought attention and she had mood swings when having her monthly period, but especially at special events and occasions she was calmer this term. We resumed in the spring term, in January 2003.

Session 14 – 16 January 2003

Dora is perfect in healing. Sits quietly, still, is receptive. She needs to feel 'enclosed' to give her a thicker skin and to feel at peace. Good session.

Session 16 – 23 January 2003

She was 'under the weather' and had a bit of a cold, and didn't really manage the session well. Therefore I cut it short so that it wouldn't be a 'failure' for her.

Session 18 – 30 January 2003

A very windy day. Dora was rather giggly today so I stopped the session soon after starting. Disappointing, but there we are. Better to stop than to carry on with an unsatisfactory situation.

Instead of taking Dora usually twice a week, as I had been doing, I reduced the sessions to weekly, which she managed better.

Session 21 – 17 February 2003

Dora was very 'out of herself' and 'over the top' at lunchtime. (We had a visitor – an Inspector – for lunch; and she also has her period!) However, by contrast in the healing session she was calm, quiet and sensible.

There was one week of half-term and then we continued our weekly sessions.

Session 22 – 3 March 2003

She managed the session well. A little bit of giggling, but nothing much.

The main thing is to allay her anxieties and help bring her to peace and stillness.

Session 27 – 3 April 2003

Very 'out of herself' and volatile at lunchtime. However, very proper, calm and still in this shorter, extra session today.

For this spring term Dora's teacher said she was doing 'extremely well', and that there were no fusses, crying, or nonsense in school. Moreover 'her anxiety levels were as low as they had ever been.' Her housemother reported, however, that Dora's sense of security 'fluctuates as before', but also said that it had been possible to ask Dora to go or return from school *on her own* on certain occasions, instead of needing the added security of adult accompaniment.

In the summer term we continued to have co-operative, mainly still, quiet and contained, healing sessions. After the long summer break, we started again in the new school year.

Session 36 – 8 September 2003

Dora was whiny at lunch today (she had a sore throat last Friday).

In the session she was still, quiet and co-operative. She said 'thank you' for the healing afterwards.

Session 37 – 15 September 2003

Dora was very upset at lunchtime, tearful and didn't eat (very unusual!).

In our session she was quiet and composed. Apparently she has various fears and worries again at present.

Once again it was rather striking to see how, in the special space of a healing session, Dora could find that quietness and composure which she very much lacked at other times in the day.

Session 39 – 6 October 2003

Dora was co-operative and composed in the session, and she seems to enjoy it. It is a peaceful time for her.

I asked her if she would like to have healing twice weekly if I could do it. She said she would.

Session 41 – 10 November 2003

Took Dora for healing as usual. She managed well in spite of various external distractions today! A loud aeroplane went over, and a workman was banging away at the roof repair.

Session 43 – 24 November 2003

Rather 'high' at lunchtime today. (Has her period I believe.) However, she managed well in healing.

When I ask her how the healing feels she says, 'relaxed and tickly'.

Session 45 – 8 December 2003

I have a clear expectation for Dora in the session – to sit still and quietly – and, with a few gentle verbal reminders, she does this well. It provides a peaceful, relaxing, space for her. She says that it relaxes her.

Christmas comes again, and holidays!

In the New Year 2004 we continued our sessions through the spring term, though she missed some through having the 'flu and then a rash.

Session 50 – 1 March 2004

Co-operated well in healing today. She says it makes her feel 'safe and relaxed'.

This was a feeling she continued to express verbally also in the summer term.

Session 53 – 17 May 2004

Dora was co-operative in healing. Sat still, peaceful, quiet. I remind her of the helpful image (visualisation) of her being covered and protected by a dark blue cloak. She went back to class, alone, after the session.

When I saw her at break-time she said she felt 'relaxed'.

Session 55 – 28 June 2004

Still and peaceful in healing today. She said she felt 'safe and relaxed' when I had my hands on her feet.

Judging by how Dora responded in the healing sessions and what she said when I asked her how she felt, I had the clear impression that the healing was of definite benefit to her. Certainly it did provide, again and again, an oasis of peacefulness.

Her school report for 2003–2004 referred to Dora's growing confidence, and her reduced anxiety. She had apparently had a 'good year' in school. Her housemother noted that Dora was now more able to verbalise and express her feelings, rather than simply reacting to them. She could say when she felt angry or upset about something. It was also acknowledged that Dora needed 'spaces when she could become quiet and peaceful'.

We were able to resume sessions in the new school year in the long autumn term.

Session 56 – 6 September 2004

Dora was co-operative and receptive. She was actually already in the room and sat down before I arrived.

I asked Dora two or three times what she felt when my hands were in different positions, e.g. over the heart area (not touching). She said 'safe, warm', but over the solar plexus/stomach area she said it made her 'feel sick'.

She sat quietly and still in the session.

Session 57 – 13 September 2004

Again co-operative, still, quiet, receptive. She mentioned about the invisible cloak that we talked about last term. She prefers a green one, a cloak that is protective and strong.

In the healing session Dora doesn't rock (rocking is one of her characteristic behaviours). I asked her twice what she felt in the session. She said, 'safe and relaxing'.

Session 61 – 14 October 2004

She came into Chalice in a silly way saying a worker's name repeatedly. I asked her to sit on the bench in the entrance to become quiet first, which she did.

In the session she managed well. Became giggly once but I pointed out to her that we could only continue if she was sensible.

So, a peaceful session.

At the end we spoke again about her purple/green cloak which is invisible and strong, and which can keep her safe and sound.

She then had to walk to Cinnabar by herself.

We also continued our healing after the two-week autumn half-term.

Session 64 – 11 November 2004

Dora was settled and peaceful in this session. I asked her to sit still and try not to move at all – including her fingers!

She mentioned again about her purple/green cloak, and I reminded her that as soon as she thought of it in the morning it would be there, helping her to be safe and sound.

Session 69 – 2 December 2004

No music today. Dora managed very well without the music and also without having her plastic horse in her bag, which she had forgotten and which there-fore worried her.

I reminded her to sit still and to be very quiet and, with this support, there was indeed some real peace and quiet. I told her that she had done very well.

This was the last session with Dora who was then 15 years old. She was of course still emotionally sensitive and anxious but thanks to many curative inputs she was making observable progress in her maturing and growing up.

Although healing sessions were only once or twice a week and of short duration, perhaps 20 minutes on average, Dora had been able to have them regularly over a two-year period. As she had herself often described them as helping her to feel 'safe and relaxed', there is good rea-son to think that they were beneficial towards her personal development and progress especially in view of her very vulnerable and anxious disposition.

Alan, diagnosed with autism

Alan had an uneventful birth and he seemed to be a 'normal' baby, apart from being rather passive. However, his early history showed that his motor development was late. He only sat up unaided at around 13 months and did not achieve walking until aged two. Although he was said to have first spoken at the normal age he then 'lost' the words he had previously acquired and no longer used speech as a means of communica-tion. Indeed he appeared to lack the motivation to communicate, though he seemed to 'understand everything' and, as he grew older, he remained an 'aloof' child who was seemingly indifferent to others. Already at two years of age Alan did not look at people, but showed repetitive patterns of behaviour such as lining up his toys. Alan later received a diagnosis of autism, which was probably of the classic Kanner's Syndrome type. He was physically quite able at most things, but lacked self-motivation.

Previously I had worked therapeutically with Alan on a one-to-one basis, before taking him specifically for healing sessions in November 2002 when he was then around 18 years old. He was a good-looking young man, with a largish head.

Session 1 – 14 November 2002

I fetched Alan from Cinnabar (the seniors building), at the start of their break-time.

He took some prompting before he got up to come. He walked with me, his head turned downwards and twiddling his hair. But he *did* keep walking all the way; he didn't stop or get 'stuck'.

In healing Alan was co-operative and he came in and sat on the chair straightaway.

When he went back afterwards he was more 'open' – head not down as before and not twiddling his hair. (But this might have been the incentive of tea break at last?!)

Session 2 – 5 December 2002

Alan came with me willingly.

He shredded some leaves on the way to Chalice.

He was still and partly relaxed in the session, and his eyes were closed quite a bit. Not holding his breath much, I think.

Session 3 – 12 December 2002

Alan came to Chalice and first needed the toilet.

He didn't really relax in healing today, nor does he look happy. He gives the impression of someone who just doesn't feel at ease and comfortable in his body. He hasn't really taken hold of it. When is Alan most happy?

After the Christmas holidays we continued in the New Year.

Session 4 – 16 January 2003

Alan walks scraping his feet over the earth, or shuffling, you could say. Inclined forward with his head and upper body.

He was OK in the session. Not entirely closed off visually (he had his eyes closed only part of the time).

I feel, rightly or wrongly, that he's willed himself to close off over the years, for whatever reason(s).

He needs warming through, especially in the middle, heart-sphere, and down into his legs. His knees were cold.

When Alan had come in he had taken off his coat and hung it up by the loop – showing he is aware and skilful.

Session 6 – 30 January 2003

I came earlier for him today, arriving during tea break in Cinnabar. I also took him back to Cinnabar after the session.

Alan had his eyes open a good deal of the time. He still very much gives me the impression of being uncomfortable in his body. However, he is not holding his breath in the same marked way he used to do some years ago. Well, he is amenable to me placing my hands on him, and I hope it helps!

Session 8 – 13 February 2003

Alan seemed much more peaceful and relaxed today. He was not twiddling his hair.

He looked at me directly at times, and at other times kept his eyes closed. He was breathing a little quickly – by this I mean short, shallow breaths – but not holding his breath.

Alan gives very much a 'head' impression, as if his head has his body attached rather than really having taken hold of the rest of his body.

At the end of the session he got up and went out and put his coat on. He made no attempt to do up the zip, so I asked him if he wanted me to help him and he indicated this verbally, not actually forming words, but clearly giving verbal affirmation.

The spring half-term arrived.

Session 9 – 6 March 2003

A co-operative session with Alan. Why no speech? He seemed reasonably relaxed – or at least not too uptight!

Session 11 – 27 March 2003

He doesn't reveal much! However, Alan was looking at me when, for example, I worked on his legs and feet. Could he speak if he tried, or wanted to? His breathing, in terms of holding it in, is not so pronounced as it used to be.

Session 12 – 3 April 2003

Closed off today. Eyes shut, head bent down. I tend to feel that he chooses to close off (but I might be wrong). So I did the session and can only hope he gets some benefit, but it is not obvious to me that he does.

I saw Alan in his house on one day. His housemother had told me that he had come back in a 'manic state' from the farm. Screaming, taking his clothes off, and agitated.

Session 13 – 7 April 2002

I gave him some healing in his room.

Certainly Alan was 'wide awake', looking at me directly. No closed, cast-down eyes today. He put on the CD *he* wanted, having selected it from the pile. His movements and hearing were different from the way he normally scuffs and drags himself around.

Apparently he has been behaving differently since his visit to a college, just over a week ago.

Session 14 – 10 April 2003

Once again in the healing room in Chalice, Alan was sat quietly with his eyes closed, but not squeezed together as if 'shutting off'.

He is not so closed off as he has been. A couple of times he, of his own initiative, inclined towards me as I had my hands over his chest and back areas.

Session 15 – 22 May 2003

He was nearly dropping off to sleep in the session. Eyes closed. (Apparently he had little, if any, sleep last night.) At the end of the session I tickled him and he woke up! He looked very directly at me. I took Alan to his house, where he hung up his coat. He sat in the sitting room and *he* took a map book to look through. Awake again!

Session 16 – 25 June 2003

I saw Alan today. He was quiet and co-operative. (I'm told that in the house he's in a good state, singing and cheerful.)

His legs look thin, and altogether he gives a fairly lean impression.

He will be going on to college in the summer.

Session 17 – 9 July 2003

I saw Alan in Cinnabar today, in the classroom.

Apparently he'd been rather 'manic' in the morning. Now he was just resting, head down on a desk, with music quietly on. So I gave him some healing where he was. His head remained down, so I didn't see his face today.

Alan did leave us, and some years later I heard that he was getting on quite well. As with other children and young people with autism, it can remain an enigma as to why they are unable or, perhaps, sometimes unwilling, to use some potentials which they seem to possess and which, in unguarded moments, can shine through in surprising ways.

In the book, *Autism – A Holistic Approach* (Woodward and Hogenboom 2002), there is presented an anthroposophical perspective on autism and ways to help alleviate this condition. However, we should remember that even when children have received the same Autistic Spectrum diagnosis it is still a matter of building a therapeutic relationship with *each individual child* and seeing how responsive he or she is to what is being offered. We will notice this concretely in the case studies which now follow.

Diagnostically, it is also important to try to ascertain from the developmental history if a child is showing a 'primary' or rather a 'secondary' form of autism. For example, a secondary autism can arise when there is a primary developmental communication problem, such as an aphasia. If the aphasic condition is recognised and alleviated, the accompanying autistic features may also then considerably recede.

Trevor, diagnosed with autism, mild cerebral palsy and aphasia

Trevor also had a diagnosis of autism. Although Trevor did show some typical autistic behaviour patterns, including avoiding eye contact and getting upset by any changes in routine, and obsessions such as spinning things, rocking himself and twiddling bits of thread in front of his eyes, he also had other difficulties.

He was a sickly baby and at six months had his first seizure, followed by further infantile spasms. At 18 months he had his first Grand Mal epileptic seizure. His developmental milestones were all delayed and he only walked at around two and a half years of age, and there was no speech at all. However, his hearing was all right and he liked music and songs.

Trevor had tantrums when he could not get his own way, and he would also bang his head on the sharpest surface available. Unlike many classically autistic children he did not have good balance, but was rather movement disturbed. Other diagnoses included mild cerebral palsy and aphasia.

I began one-to-one healing sessions with Trevor when he was 16 years old. This was the first of a total of 65 sessions given over two school years, and therefore I must again be selective in sharing our sessions with you.

Session 1 – 13 May 2002

Trevor was with three other peers listening to the piano being played in the school's movement hall.

I therefore gave him some healing there, as he was sat still and quiet and attentive to the music. When S., a helper, had finished playing the piece of music, Trevor indicated through gestures and sounds that he wanted to hear more, and so S. resumed playing.

Under these helpful and relaxing conditions Trevor was completely co-operative to receiving hands-on healing.

He has no speech, is movement disturbed, epileptic and autistic. However, of the four pupils present he was clearly the most attentive and appreciative of the music.

Session 2 – 16 May 2002

He ran down to Chalice! In my room he listened to taped music. Trevor sat peacefully and I worked mostly from behind him. He allowed me to hold his hands. He got off the chair and moved to another chair twice, but this was no problem. A good session. No banging of his hand or arms on the chair and no noises.

Trevor was someone who would sometimes bang his hands or arms very hard on the sides of a chair. Although this looked very demonstrative and forceful when it occurred, he didn't appear to register any pain or discomfort when doing it. Fortunately it rarely happened in our healing sessions.

Session 3 – 20 May 2002

Trevor was still and peaceful during the healing. Not fiddling with his hands. He sat cross-legged and kept his shoes on.

Peaceful, attentive and appears relaxed.

'Open' and receptive – probably enjoys the music.

Session 4 – 23 May 2002

Trevor came down with me to Chalice, loping along as he does.

In healing he loosened his boots, but didn't take them off as such so they were still on his feet. He took a thread from his sock to twiddle and chew. However, he became still and peaceful in the session, holding his own hands still.

Co-operative and receptive. He didn't get up from the chair at all.

Session 5 – 27 May 2002

A remarkable session for its calmness. Trevor sat still on the chair, legs down, shoes on. He was very still and peaceful.

He got up just once to go over to the tape recorder – touched it – then came and sat down. He made no sound throughout the session.

Session 6 – 30 May 2002

Trevor took off his boots and socks in the entrance to Chalice before going into my room. This was *his* initiative and not a requirement from me.

He sat cross-legged on the chair and sat quietly listening to the music. When the tape ended, he got off his chair to show me that he wanted the music to continue.

Trevor tolerates touch – also on his head. He was peaceful and still during the session. (He was lively coming down to the session and also going back – walking along in his rocking back and forth fashion.)

Session 8 – 10 June 2002

A very good session. Trevor was still, quiet, attentive, peaceful.

He sat properly on the chair, his hands under his legs. (To keep them still presumably?) Shoes on. Feet crossed. Sits upright.

Undoubtedly he likes the music. If the music wasn't on he might not be so still and peaceful but, at any rate, he is receptive to the healing. Also he doesn't mind me putting my hands lightly on his head.

Trevor makes eye-to-eye contact after the session. Altogether I am impressed how 'together' he can be.

He doesn't speak – but can he still learn this at all?

I definitely feel that the session provides a peaceful, relaxed space for him.

Trevor's housemother told me that his parents had been pleased with his week's half-term at home. They had found him to be quite calm. So this is positive.

Session 9 – 17 June 2002

Trevor is remarkable in the sessions.

He sits still and properly. Obviously the music captures him, but he is also willing to receive touch and healing. It is impressive to see what a peaceful, contained, picture he gives.

He also can make good eye-to-eye contact, as he did at the end of today's session.

Session 12 – 1 July 2002

He's really my star pupil in being at peace, quiet and stillness!

Of course he likes the music. Whether he would be so quiet and peaceful without it I don't know. At any event, that he can sit still and be calm and peaceful is a blessing.

Session 14 – 4 July 2002

I took Trevor for a short session today. He obviously likes to come to this, to listen to the music! Whilst the music is playing he is totally amenable to me placing my hands on him – including his head.

In that Trevor is at peace, quiet and stillness, there is obvious benefit to him entering into such a space.

Session 16 – 11 July 2002

Took Trevor this morning. When the music stops he gets up, probably to switch it back on. Whilst the music plays he is still, quiet and at rest. This allows for me to place my hands on him with his compliance.

Trevor often sits with his hands under his legs, or else holding his hands.

Outside of the session it is incredible to see how he moves! There is no normality at all about his walking – arms are in restless movements and he lopes along. On the other hand he can also, at times, stand still.

The session clearly provides him with a space to be peaceful in and to relax. (Does he have any fits? I've not seen them. But why does he sometimes screw his eyes with his hands?)

The summer holidays intervened. We began again in the new school year in September 2002.

In the case of Trevor in particular, it is clear that the background music was a great asset in helping him to come to quietness and stillness. Indeed someone might argue that it was primarily the pleasant music, rather than the spiritual healing which provided for him the calmness and beneficial value of the sessions. I did not, however, choose to 'experiment' with this situation by, for example, either having no music playing, or switching it off at some point, to see how Trevor would react to this. As far as I was concerned, with the music on, Trevor showed himself to be very willing and receptive to hands-on healing and I could not ask for more. It was the quality of each session which was of first importance to me, rather than trying to determine experimentally which of the two factors, healing or music, was having the strongest influence on him.

Indeed for all the pupils I had for healing sessions, I felt that the pleasant, relaxing music helped to provide an environment conducive to spiritual healing practice, and that this was its sole purpose. The more calm and relaxed a child was, the more receptive they could be to receiving healing.

In fact, after using taped music in this way for approximately three years, in the fourth year of healing practice I dispensed with it altogether and found that a more profound experience of peace and stillness was possible with the pupils I then took for healing.

Trevor's housemother reported that during that summer term Trevor had sometimes woken up early in the morning and was very noisy. However, as the term went on, he slept well and was no longer disturbed in the morning.

He was having no other special therapies in addition to healing that term.

Session 17 – 2 September 2002

Trevor of course sits still because of the music and, with the music playing, he is totally co-operative to me placing my hands on him.

He took his shoes and socks off before he came in. Trevor will sit with his legs down if I indicate this to him. Otherwise he's quite comfortable to sit cross-legged on the chair.

His housemother tells me that Trevor is a bit restless in the house at mealtimes, but that he sleeps all right.

Session 18 – 9 September 2002

Trevor came into Chalice noisily and with vigour!

However, in the session he was peaceful, quiet and I would say 'centred' and at rest.

It is impressive just how responsive he is to the session. In fact at the end, when the music had stopped, he was quite content to sit there quietly – he didn't jump up to put more music on, but just sat.

Session 21 – 19 September 2002

I took Trevor today, as I had a spare session going. It was, however, only short, about ten minutes or so as Trevor got up after this time and clearly indicated he wanted the music off, and that he was ready to finish.

I have not had this with Trevor before and I don't know the reason for this, but during the healing he was quiet and peaceful as usual.

Session 24 – 30 September 2002

Trevor came willingly to the session.

He took off his shoes and socks and also his outside jacket.

He was peaceful during the healing. Then, later, he started rubbing his eyes as he can sometimes.

Shortly after that he deliberately started to turn over the chairs in the room, also the stool! I did not become cross with him, but I held his wrists to prevent him doing more. He was not making any agitated noises at all.

I righted the chairs, sat him back down, and then helped to put on his shoes and socks, and finished the healing peacefully.

Trevor has never reacted like this before in this room. Why now? What was stirred in him to do this? What was he showing? Had he simply wanted the session to end? If so he could simply have gone to turn off the music.

Healing can of course work strongly, and I did feel the healing was strong this morning.

Session 25 – 7 October 2002

Trevor was still and quiet and peaceful in this session. There was no repeat of upturning the chairs as he had, out of the blue, a week before.

Trevor's housemother reported that in the first three weeks of the autumn term, in September, he had been 'quite disturbed', but that he is better now. Moreover, when he is in a good mood there is 'more eye contact and smiles'.

The two weeks autumn half-term came, and then we resumed in November.

Session 26 – 4 November 2002

Trevor was co-operative. At times he rubbed his eyes with his hands – vigorously as he does. However, he put his hands down through my coaxing.

Peaceful, quiet, when music is on, and then also perfectly willing for physical contact.

However, I still use a certain *indirect* approach in order not to confront him too strongly.

Again he took off his shoes and socks before coming in.

Session 31 – 9 December 2002

Trevor was again at peace and quiet in the session. Sometimes he intentionally looks towards me – once in this session.

Towards the end he 'screwed' his eyes, as he does sometimes. I believe he likes and takes pleasure in the sessions.

At the end of the autumn term his housemother reported that Trevor 'has been very good, less noisy', and also that he could 'take initiative by himself'.

We continued on in the New Year, 2003.

Session 32 – 20 January 2003

I was still busy with E., another pupil, when Trevor opened the door ready to come in! So I finished with E. first.

Trevor was quiet, peaceful, still. He made no attempt to take off his shoes, and he also sat with his feet down on the floor.

Several times he looked at me and made *direct eye contact* – his initiative.

Certainly the healing, with the music on, provides a quiet and peaceful space for him.

At the end he wasn't in any hurry to get up and leave.

Session 33 – 27 January 2003

Had a session with Trevor today.

He didn't actually turn to make any direct eye contact today. However, he took the initiative to get up after 20 minutes to switch off the music – he had had sufficient.

Towards the end he screwed his eyes, though he's amenable when I gently lower his hands from doing this.

So I hope he received what he needed.

Session 36 – 17 February 2003

Trevor had a very short session today. Very unusual – because after about five minutes he got up and clearly indicated that the music be switched off and that he was ready to leave!

Why he acted like this I don't know. However, since he was so definite, I complied with his wishes and walked him back to Cinnabar.

The spring half-term was just one week, and afterwards his teacher told me that Trevor's parents had had a very good time with him at home. Our sessions then continued in the same very positive and receptive vein during the rest of the spring term. After the three weeks Easter holiday we resumed once again.

Session 43 – 12 May 2003

Trevor was quiet, still, peaceful in the session. Not screwing his eyes. Stayed for the full length of the session.

Session 45 – 26 May 2003

Co-operative in the session until he comes to the point of screwing his eyes. Once started, he repeats this.

He showed when he'd had enough by getting up and indicating that the music be switched off, after about 20 minutes.

Session 47 – 23 June 2003

Trevor was very calm and peaceful today. Did a bit of eye-screwing at one point, but also stopped it again.

He was in no rush to go at the end of the session. In fact I had finished the healing so we just sat and listened to the music.

Session 50 – 14 July 2003

Last session this term. Trevor was peaceful and co-operative.

I was glad to have a good session, as last Thursday he had become very upset in religion lesson and I had to take him out.

The long summer holidays began. It was good to hear by the end of them that Trevor had had a good holiday at home and that he was more manageable, co-operative and mature. We made a fresh start in the new school year in the autumn term.

Session 51 – 8 September 2003

Trevor was picking his socks and eating the threads in the session – something he hasn't done before (maybe he was just hungry!). Apart from that, he co-operated, was quiet and sat on the stool.

He's had a sequence of fits during the last couple of days and stayed in his house. This was, I understand, an unusual occurrence.

Session 52 – 15 September 2003

He was fine in this session. Quiet, still, co-operative, and not eating his socks.

Trevor seems settled again after his run of fits last week.

Session 54 – 6 October 2003

Trevor was co-operative in the session and he allows me to touch him. He did pull some threads from his sock to chew on.

A positive session I would say.

Is he vocalising more I wonder? On the way to his house he was making some sounds and noises.

The autumn half-term gave us a break for two weeks.

Session 55 – 3 November 2003

Trevor came straight after his seniors eurythmy lesson. He was co-operative and peaceful. He did take off his shoes and socks himself. A couple of times, or was it only once, he turned to look at me directly.

Session 56 – 10 November 2003

Another positive session with Trevor. He sat still and was receptive.

Only put his hands/fingers to 'screw' his eyes at the end.

He looked at me very deliberately, certainly once.

His housemother came into Chalice when we had finished and *I saw Trevor smile.* I think he makes good contact with people he knows.

Trevor's housemother told me today that recently Trevor has done two quite new things: he took her hand and put it to his head and her other hand to stroke his cheek; and he listened and responded when his mother spoke to him on the phone. She was deeply impressed by these quite new events!

Session 59 – 1 December 2003

Again Trevor made a point of looking at me directly. He turns his head towards me to do this.

Quiet and co-operative. He folded his arms in this session.

We resumed healing in the New Year, 2004.

Session 60 – 19 January 2004

The first session this term – this year!

Trevor was receptive and co-operative. Sits quietly and still. No eye rubbing. Looked at me again in the session – makes contact.

Seems quite comfortable with the session.

Session 62 – 2 February 2004

Had a normal-length session with Trevor today. He looked at me, turned to do so in the session. After the session was also smiling – he looked pleased.

We continued after the short half-term.

Session 64 – 1 March 2004

An interesting session!

He took off his shoes and socks before.

Looked at me very directly several times. Sat quietly, hands folded, legs crossed. When I went down to his feet he appeared to find this amusing, and laughed in his own way.

He also got hiccups towards the end. Seemed cheerful.

Session 65 – 8 March 2004

Trevor was not his usual self today. Was eating threads from his jumper sleeve. Didn't turn to look at me once.

So he was in a withdrawn state, and not receptive as usual, for whatever reason. I suppose we all have our off days!

This was actually our last session. I believe that healing was really beneficial to Trevor judging by his consistently relaxed and peaceful state in our sessions observed over a two-year period. Of course the actual degree of help, support, comfort and peace it gave him is difficult to estimate, and we don't know how he would have been if he hadn't received regular healing sessions.

However, for a young man on the Autistic Spectrum it was particularly impressive to see the increased direct eye contact which Trevor made with me in the sessions, and also his occasional smiling. This, together with his housemother's observations in November 2003, suggested that new and positive developments were taking place in his interpersonal relationships with others.

Trevor left the school at Easter 2004. His parents felt he had matured a lot, was generally more co-operative and contained, and more adult-like. However, he still required constant supervision at home, and so they were seeking a 52-week placement for him in order to alleviate the 'challenges' of school holidays for everyone concerned. At Trevor's age, this was no doubt a sensible and realistic change to make.

Mark, diagnosed with autism

Mark had also received a diagnosis of autism and with it severe learning difficulties, possibly originating from early experiences of neglect in infancy. However, little was known of his earliest development.

His behaviour and moods were very changeable and, when stressed, he exhibited self-injurious behaviours such as pulling his own hair. He had certain habitual mannerisms including flicking pages, tapping objects, and a preoccupation with water.

Mark was delayed in his receptive and expressive language though, fortunately, he had speech. He could become very anxious, particularly at night, and had difficulty getting to sleep. He had no awareness of danger. Mark also had some gastro-intestinal problems, with not very regular bowel movements. Over a period of time he had been on a large number of different medications in an effort to control his emotional behavioural difficulties, but unfortunately with very little success. Consequently his parents had tried a number of complementary therapy approaches and were also very open to him receiving spiritual healing from me when he was 15 years old. No background music was played in our sessions.

Session 1 – 26 September 2005

The first session with Mark went well – as well as I could have hoped! He sat on the stool throughout the session.

For the healing I put my hands on Mark's shoulders standing behind him; he allowed this. I then put my right hand over his head whilst putting my left over his chest area. I then sat on the right-hand chair with my right hand on his back and the left hand over his heart area. Mark spent some time examining my left hand – I let him do this.

He seemed quite 'happy', interested, in what he was doing. He made contact by taking my hand and fingers. I stayed in this side-on position throughout the rest of the session, and Mark seemed quite 'at home', comfortable, with this.

At no time did he object to receiving hands-on contact and I had the impression he was pretty still and receptive.

I didn't spend much time with my hands over his head, nor did I go along his spine, nor on his feet. I felt it was more important to do what he was 'comfortable' with in this first session.

Mark made some direct contact, looking at me, and he also smiled. He wasn't in any rush to leave when we had finished healing.

So from the point of view of his co-operation, a very successful session, I would say. Mark did speak at various points in the session, but I couldn't understand all that he said.

Session 2 – 28 September 2005

A very interesting session and different in various ways from the first one.

Soon after he came into the room Mark said, in his almost whispering way, that he wanted the toilet. I asked E., a helper, to take him.

When he returned to the room he did not sit down on the stool. Rather he was up and about, and he opened the window (which I shut again).

After a time Mark came and sat on the chair, rather than the stool. So I did the healing with him on the chair, where he remained throughout the session.

A striking thing today was the large amount of *contact* Mark made – both by looking at me, at times with smiles, and also by making *his own* hands-on contact. In fact whilst I was giving him healing he was holding my hand, the right one, most of the time.

I did not go through the normal hands-on procedure with all the hand positions, but rather worked *with* him with what seemed most acceptable to him. Mainly I had my hands on his chest and upper back areas.

Mark co-operated in his own way. He seemed quite happy with the session, and he was not rejecting hands-on contact – indeed he himself was making it with me! He was far more active and restless today, though there were also times when he sat peacefully.

Session 3 – 3 October 2005

Mark sat down at once on the stool. He didn't wish to explore the room it seems.

The outstanding feature of this session was his restlessness! He was moving his hands on his left leg.

He allowed me to make hands-on contact with him. I was able to do various hand placements: on his shoulders, chest and back; on/over his head; on his feet.

Because of his restlessness I went down to his feet, hoping to help 'ground' him and settle him down. In this position I had also a lot of direct eye-to-eye contact with him. He made ready and 'open' contact, and he did come to stillness for a time.

Towards the end of the session (20 minutes), he was still and much calmer.

Session 4 – 5 October 2005

Another interesting session. Mark was much less restless today.

There was more peacefulness about Mark today and there were times, albeit briefly, when I could just place my hand on his chest without him fingering and examining it!

He appeared to be in a happy frame of mind. At times smiles and some eye contact also. I don't find that he avoids eye contact and in fact he is very willing to make contact, both physically and face-to-face.

The healing was mainly from behind him, or sat at his side. I feel he is receptive and is not rejecting it.

He seems to be sensitive to hands on his head, though I did manage to do this over his head to some extent.

He strikes me as awake and aware. Friendly and co-operative in the session, even though somewhat obsessive about fingering/examining my hand. Twenty minutes.

The next session with Mark was restless and he did not remain sitting on the stool throughout, but got up half-way through the session and healing could then not be continued. Before this he was receptive and still for a time, and all through the session he seemed happy enough and was quite talkative, speaking in a whisper.

Session 6 – 12 October 2005

This was certainly the best session to date! Mark sat on the stool throughout and he was very peaceful. I felt he was more 'centred', and I was able to go through most of the usual hand placements.

He was very co-operative, calm, peaceful and I would say relaxed.

He's sensitive over his head (he *always* wears a cap); I put my hand *over* his head rather than touching it.

I received detailed reports from house and school, and also from his parents for the two-week autumn half-term at home. For example, his parents had found him to be less anxious and more secure and confident. They reported that Mark had been co-operative and helpful and 'really connected to us; we noticed huge advances in this area'. His parents also remarked that Mark was able to walk past a dog which was not on a lead, whereas previously he would have been petrified!

At school, in the house, there had been fewer tempers and they were less severe. He had been quicker to get up and get dressed in the morning, and quicker to start eating. Mark also had daily bowel movements for six days in a row, which was most unusual.

In school he was more active than before, for example, in participating in woodwork lessons. In the six healing sessions, seen as a series, his restlessness had decreased over time.

We resumed again in November.

Session 7 — 16 November 2005

He came in and sat on the stool and he stayed there until nearly the end of the session, when he moved onto a chair.

Mark was restless throughout the session today. Hardly for a second was he still, mainly with restless hands and arms.

He seemed quite happy to be in the healing session as such. He wasn't protesting at all, nor was he distressed.

It would be a real breakthrough if he could really sit still for *any* time!

He leant towards me again when I sat beside him, and he also looked at me at times.

The next session with Mark was also very restless, but the ninth one was different.

Session 9 — 23 November 2005

The session today was very different from the last one. Much more settled and peaceful.

He didn't take my hand once today to examine it but was biting the fingernails of his own hand, and this was the main activity of restlessness. His legs were still. Bodily he was much less restless than in the last session.

He spoke at times, but it's difficult for me to understand what he says. It sounded like 'playing'.

When I was on the chair beside him *he moved and leant closer to me*. In fact he seemed to want and to be comfortable with this very close physical contact.

Hand positions were on shoulders to begin, then along his spine but *he indicated where he would allow this by moving my hands*. I tried again *over his head with one hand and this worked for a while but he's immediately aware of the physical contact to his head, and moves away from this.

At one point, well into the session, he seemed to get a bit disturbed. This was shown by the unusually deep sounds he made as his speech is nearly always whispered.

I asked him if he was all right and he calmed again. He also smiled at me later.

Mark seemed receptive to healing, on his terms, so to speak. I spent a lot of time on heart and solar plexus areas – both front and back.

At the end of the session he was in no hurry to leave the room. There was again eye-to-eye contact.

In the following session Mark was rather obsessively biting his nails and it was very difficult for him to keep his hands still. Once again he leant towards me in the side-on heart position, and he seemed comfortable and receptive with this physical contact.

E. told me that Mark had had a 'good week with sleeping and toileting': two very important areas in his life.

Session 11 – 30 November 2005

I cannot say this was a quiet session, but it was a very interesting one!

Mark was speaking a lot, saying the same thing repeatedly, which sounded to me like 'aeroplane'. It became very clear as the session went on that he was speaking about an aeroplane in connection with his 'Daddy'. (He actually said, 'Hello Daddy' to me when he came in.)

Mark sat on the stool throughout and only got up when he'd had enough, which was anyway near the end of our time. He appeared to get disturbed and upset a number of times, and he spoke then with a very deep voice.

Actually Mark co-operated well and he allowed hands-on contact, even though he was expressing himself emotionally. I actually felt there was a lot of contact being made, as he was looking at me and telling me of his wishes ('aeroplane', 'Daddy'), and communicating. The depth in his voice when he's agitated stands in such contrast to his usual whispered voice.

Interestingly in spite of him expressing himself in this demonstrative way, I felt that the session went well. He had the opportunity to let it out. I talked to him to ask him what he meant, and also to reassure him. Perhaps he felt safe enough with me to express these emotions?

(Healing can of course also come about through a release of emotions and not only through peace and quiet.)

Over these five sessions since the autumn half-term there had been quite a lot of restlessness. On the other hand he hadn't wanted out, but was quite willing to be in the sessions and to allow hands-on contact. There had also continued to be good eye-to-eye contact, smiling, leaning towards me and touching my hand.

Again I received some detailed reports from house, school and Mark's parents. In particular, his parents remarked that Mark seemed to be 'more in control of his emotions,' and that they had 'looked after a much more settled, connected son, over the holiday – which had been a pleasure'. Also his digestive system showed improvements; and he seemed to understand verbal requests much more easily and to respond more quickly.

In the house-life at school he started to play regularly with a young staff child, was more secure and free to move around in the house and, on a few occasions, he took the initiative. In school the most frequent comment was that Mark was calm and quiet in class for the first long lesson of the day.

We continued healing sessions in the New Year, 2006. Another series of six healing sessions was planned for the first half of the spring term; as it happened we just managed five of these.

In the first session in January 2006 Mark was very restless, constantly moving his hands and quite often his legs also, though he sat on the stool throughout. The following session had to be abandoned after a short time because Mark was being uncooperative, and I could only work with him if he showed himself willing to receive healing. He seemed to be in a rather cheeky or mischievous frame of mind. However, in the next session Mark was relatively peaceful and co-operative for some 13 minutes, but then decided to put his dirty boots up on the stool which was unacceptable behaviour. There was no eye-to-eye contact in the session.

Mark's housemother mentioned to me that there were various changes with him. He was acting more like a teenager and wanted his 'own space' in a way he hadn't before.

Session 15 – 1 February 2006

Mark came in and showed no intention of sitting down quickly in order to start. Instead he went and opened the window wide.

I made it very clear to Mark, by speaking to him, that if *he* wanted healing today he would need to sit down on the stool. And in fact he did so!

At one point he started playing up in the session, attempting to put his feet up onto the chairs. I made it clear to him, by taking his feet off the chairs, that this was not acceptable behaviour. I was ready to finish the session if he would not co-operate.

As it was he moved from the stool to a chair, and the rest of the session took place with him sat there. I kept my hands over his heart area – in front and behind. He was fiddling and moving his hands through most of the session. There were, however, some moments of stillness. I feel it is quite special when such an interlude comes – a moment of stillness and quietude in the sea of movement activity which he seems almost compelled to do.

Mark did look up at me at one point in the session and said, 'I like Daddy'. I acknowledged this and said that his Daddy also liked him.

I brought the session to a close while he was still being co-operative, after around 14 minutes.

In the next session Mark was also co-operative and receptive to receiving healing. In that sense it was a 'good' session, with also a lot of contact and communication taking place between us, quite intimate and warm. Again I spent most of the time over the heart region; he was still very sensitive about any proximity of my hands to his head.

The spring half-term came and once more I received reports about how Mark had been getting on in various situations at school, and in the half-term at home. The main impression was that he had shown increased independence and confidence.

This did not necessarily make his daily management any easier, but still it was seen as progress. There were clear signs of reduced anxiety; some initiatives; and his bowel movements had improved over the term. He had learnt new skills in practical lessons, such as basketry and wood-work, and he was more engaged in what he was doing. At home his parents felt that 'he is so much improved, 100 per cent calmer'.

After the half-term break four more sessions took place with Mark, though the first planned one had to be abandoned due to his lack of co-operation. Thereafter, though somewhat testing, Mark did show suf-ficient co-operation, willingness and receptivity for sessions to take place. In giving healing to such a young man with very special needs, there is no doubt that the ability of a healer is sorely tried in the sense of needing to remain inwardly calm and unruffled no matter what happens! The last session with Mark did not take place in the healing room, in which he would not settle down, but outside on the bench near to Chalice.

Session 20 – 22 March 2006

Mark sat down on the bench and there he settled down with me sat next to him. I gave him healing, hands on upper back/neck and on the heart area. I even put my hand over his head (he was again wearing his cap), without him pulling away from this. I also spoke to him.

Mark was able in this way to receive healing for around ten minutes. He was not silly or restless in this situation. Eventually I told him it was break-time.

It is sometimes necessary to be very flexible in one's approach and way of 'delivering' healing to pupils with special needs and challenging behaviours. Provided the child is willing to receive healing, as is shown in his or her behaviours, then the healer can also be willing to 'bend over backwards' in order to give what is needed.

Mark was a very likeable young man who needed, and received, a great deal of support in all areas of his life at the school, particularly on the part of those who lived with him on a daily basis.

From the observations which I received from others it was clear that Mark was changing and progressing in the course of this school year, particularly in the areas of increased independence and confidence.

Wendy, diagnosed with Autistic Spectrum Disorder

If Mark was generally restless in healing sessions and his behaviour at times testing, Wendy was the complete opposite. She was still, quiet, totally co-operative and receptive.

Like Mark, Trevor and Alan, Wendy also had an Autistic Spectrum diagnosis. As a baby she had demanded a lot of attention from her mother. She only walked unaided at nearly three years of age, and her language development included a lot of repetitions and echolalia. By age four and a half she was considered to have 'mild' learning difficulties, but these were then regarded as 'moderate' by age six, and 'severe' by nine years of age. Later she went to a school for autistic children.

Wendy had a high degree of anxiety, and she showed marked obsessive and compulsive behaviours. There was a history of temper outbursts, attributed to her high anxiety levels, and these had resulted in some physical harm to family, others and herself. She was, however, articulate, could read and write, enjoyed the company of others, and could be a bright and cheerful pupil. Wendy had made some good progress in having individual eurythmy therapy a little time before I took her for healing sessions in November 2003, when she was nearly 18 years old.

Session 1 – 6 November 2003

I saw Wendy in her house about 11.30am; she had been slow in getting up this morning. I told her that her mother would like me to take her for healing sessions and that I looked forward to seeing her in Chalice at 12.10pm. She was there on time, together with her housemother, and so we had our first session.

I explained to Wendy what I would do – just lightly touch her. She was agreeable to this and she co-operated throughout. (Her housemother stayed and observed this first session.) Wendy had a tickle in her throat which caused her to cough a bit and I gave her some water to drink.

Her hands were quite cool today. I said it would be good if she ate a good lunch to give her energy and strength.

Later I saw her housemother who told me that Wendy did eat well, and then also went down to her afternoon religion lesson. Clearly Wendy is someone who needs 'warming through' – soul-wise and physically. She is anxious, worries and gets rather – sometimes very – obsessional. I wondered if this could be an Asperger's type of Autistic Spectrum condition.

Session 2 – 10 November 2003

Wendy came down from Cinnabar, by herself, for healing. She still has a tickle in her throat. She was co-operative and receptive.

Session 4 – 20 November 2003

Completely co-operative and receptive. Sits still and doesn't mind touch contact. Rather cool hands. Peaceful. Sits a bit slouched over, not upright.

Apparently in her house she can exhibit swearing and screaming at times.

Session 6 – 27 November 2003

She is amenable and totally co-operative. Her hands were cold again.

Wendy got a fright when the tape recorder switched off with a click, but I reassured her. She seems to 'enjoy' the healing and appears quite comfortable with it.

I later saw her give John (a very autistic young man) a kiss on the cheek in the afternoon – quite touching!

Session 7 – 1 December 2003

Sits still. Is receptive and co-operative, and appears to be comfortable.

Cool hands; even quite cold.

She giggled a couple of times and said she'd dreamt of a flying snake last night. When Wendy speaks, in answer to my questions, she has a stutter – due to anxiety?

Her housemother felt that Wendy had been, on the whole, more peaceful in the house over the last few weeks.

Session 9 – 8 December 2003

Wendy sits quietly and is receptive. In view of her age and abilities I make a point of asking her if she is happy to have the healing *before* I begin.

Session 10 – 11 December 2003

Co-operative and quiet and still.

She is happy, she says, to continue next term also.

We did therefore continue after the Christmas holidays in the New Year 2004.

Session 11 – 12 January 2004

Wendy is co-operative, quiet, peaceful, receptive. She speaks hesitantly, almost with a stutter. When I asked her whether she wanted healing once or twice a week she said, 'twice'.

Has cold hands and she needs warming through.

Session 12 – 15 January 2004

Came again today. She doesn't initiate talking with me, usually. Sits quietly and is receptive. It's difficult to imagine her in a tantrum, or swearing, etc.! She appears comfortable with the sessions.

Session 13 –19 January 2004

Wendy said in school morning assembly that she likes me. I said I liked her also.

In healing, receptive, co-operative and comfortable. She has very cold hands. Sits slightly bent forward. Needs warming through.

And so we continued on through the spring term, in the same consistent and typical fashion. Her housemother told me that Wendy had changed a lot since having healing, with outbursts being much less frequent.

Session 23 – 22 March 2004

Wendy got upset after healing today.

She was perfectly composed during the healing itself. It seems that she was disturbed because she had seen a new person in the school.

Anyway her housefather who was coming out of a meeting and saw Wendy was upset, helped to reassure her. I suppose part of the problem for her are any *changes* which occur without due forewarning.

After the Easter holidays we started again in the summer term.

Session 24 – 3 May 2004

Wendy was in a giggly mood today, which wasn't a problem. (Much better to see her cheerful than distressed in any way.)

I asked her if she was happy to have healing and she said she was. She does not mind direct physical contact. She still has cold hands.

I told Wendy that I will see her once a week only, but not next week (I wanted to forewarn her of this).

Session 25 – 17 May 2004

Sat quietly and still, completely co-operative. Her hands were *warm* today, which was unusual. Her housemother tells me that Wendy is 'doing well'.

Session 26 – 31 May 2004

Came in quietly. Quiet throughout the session apart from two or three little giggles. Totally co-operative. Went out quite cheerfully.

I wrote in my notes that there is something 'stuck' about her nature – inflexible in her thinking perhaps – which I hope healing may help to loosen and free up. In an internal review it was reported that Wendy liked the healing sessions and *she* called them 'relaxation sessions'.

We made a fresh start, after the summer holidays, in the new school year.

Session 28 – 6 September 2004

Wendy came on time. Her hands were unusually warm – almost hot – today!

I asked her if she was happy to have healing, and she said she was.

She was still, quiet and co-operative.

I asked Wendy if she could feel anything when I put my hands on her shoes (feet) – she said, 'warm'. She sits a little hunched over.

Anyway a positive session, which she seems perfectly comfortable with.

Session 31 – 11 October 2004

Wendy came down whilst I was still busy with John. When I finished with John and opened the door, she was waiting to come in.

Wendy was quiet throughout the session except when I asked her how it felt when I had my hands in certain positions. She was rather preoccupied with looking at and moving her fingers. She sat a little bent over rather than upright.

When one hand was on her back 'heart area', I asked her how it felt. She said, 'warm'. When my hands were on her shoes (feet) she said it felt 'cosy'. I asked her if this was 'comfortable' and she said it was.

Wendy's hands were cool and a bit clammy. She spoke with her stutter. She asked me why Tom (the cat), died. I told her it had a heart problem.

I asked Wendy if she was happy to have healing – she said she was. She also said that next Monday there wouldn't be healing. (Quite right as I have a Council Meeting.) I confirmed that this was correct.

She gives the impression of being anxious, however, she appears happy enough to sit in the healing session and she co-operates entirely. How can healing help her? Perhaps by reducing anxiety or any obsessive behaviours? By giving reassurance and peace?

We continued our healing sessions after the autumn half-term.

Session 32 – 8 November 2004

Wendy got here later than I expected today. However, this was fine.

She seemed relaxed – not tense or agitated. She noticed that the tape recorder was different! She thought I'd bought a new one, but I told her it had come from a friend.

Wendy sits still and completely quiet for the healing. Only fiddling a bit with her fingernails. Her hands are very cold.

She doesn't mind me touching her and holding her hands. *Before* we started I had again asked her if she was happy to continue having healing once a week. She said she was.

At the end I asked her if she was all right. She said, 'yes'. She seems to be happy enough to simply come and have a quiet, peaceful, space and generally she says little.

Session 33 – 15 November 2004

An interesting session with Wendy today as she was quite talkative and also giggly at times.

I felt a lot of warmth on her back – lower back – and *over* the heart area. Her hands were cool.

Wendy remarked about my breath when I spoke close to her! Also she remarked about my lack of hair! Maybe not very tactful observations, but honest! She also said she didn't realise S. (my wife) and I were married.

I talked with Wendy also today. I think this may be helpful as usually she is very quiet and talks little.

Session 35 – 29 November 2004

She's now 19 years old.

Wendy was very quiet, still and peaceful I would say in healing. Cold hands again, but I felt warmth on her spine and head. (She has a tendency to get obsessional in her thoughts, I believe, so needs help to gain more freedom there.)

Wendy appears to like healing. I always, before I start healing, ask her if she's happy to receive it, and she replies affirmatively.

Session 37 – 6 December 2004

A very quiet session with Wendy. No music, and no sounds in Chalice apart from the regular ticking of my wall clock.

Again I asked her if she was happy to have healing and she said she was.

I asked Wendy's teacher how she was getting on. He said that since the summer something had changed in her, and she was more peaceful in herself.

I did not continue healing with Wendy in the New Year, 2005, as I had given her the choice, via her housemother, to carry on or not. I understood that she wanted to stop and, of course, I respected her wish. She left us at Easter and was at that time the oldest pupil at the school and, according to her teacher, she was maturing very well.

In the last three chapters I have been able to share with you observations from my extensive records of healing sessions with pupils who, taken together, have shown a wide range of syndromes, conditions and special needs. To do this has given me the opportunity to revisit in thought and memory these 18 very individual pupils, and I feel grateful for 'the journeys' we have together undertaken. I believe that the evidence of the sessions themselves strongly suggests that spiritual healing can often be very beneficial in creating spaces – you could almost say 'sacred spaces' – of stillness, quietness and peace. This in itself is likely to be of very real value and help to children with special needs, whatever other benefits healing may also be able to confer to each individual according to his or her very particular needs.

CHAPTER 7

Reviewing Healing Practice

I have been at some pains to point out that my practice of spiritual healing for those pupils whose parents have requested and consented to this on behalf of their children, takes place in the multi-faceted setting of the 'therapeutic community'. Pupils in this complex curative context could and did benefit from many different inputs and influences. Spiritual healing was but one of these influences.

It is therefore, I feel, of great importance not to attempt to make any outlandish or even over-optimistic claims for the positive influence or effects that healing may have provided for any individual pupil. It is far better, I believe, to be cautious and prudent than to, perhaps unjustifiably, raise false hopes for the possible benefits that spiritual healing can give to children and youngsters with special needs. However, on the other hand, one should also not ignore the clear evidence that is provided at the hand of many observations I have made over the past four years in very nearly one thousand individual healing sessions, of which a typical selection have been included in the last three chapters of this book.

This evidence attests to the fact that, again and again, and with all pupils taken for healing, a space was created in which the child or young person was enabled to come to some degree of stillness, quiet, peace and relaxation, rather like a traveller coming to a refreshing 'oasis' in the midst of a busy and sometimes demanding day. Many years of experience in curative education have shown me what a blessing, and also what a powerful curative influence it is, for a child with special needs to be helped to come to times of stillness and quietness. Even children with very restless behaviours can be helped to manage this through opportunities which are given, again and again, in the course of each new day. In a curative educational environment, such quiet spaces are in fact very deliberately created. Morning and evening prayers in the houses, graces before meals, special verses spoken in classes to start the school day and weekly non-denominational religious services, all provide good examples of such moments, or times, of stillness, quietness and peace.

Without doubt the repetition of these quiet moments has a very important, indeed indispensable, healing influence for *everyone* in a therapeutic community setting, for the adults as well as the children! Stress, tensions and frustrations can be lessened, and each person is enabled in such still moments to come more to him or herself, and to see both oneself and others in a different, clearer perspective and light, which is hardly possible if one rushes through the day from morning to evening. Or, worse still, rushes through modern life itself, with all its demands, from cradle to grave!

Certainly for over-anxious and emotionally over-sensitive children like Dora, for example, the healing sessions provided an experience of 'safety and relaxation', a place for her to become calm, more centred and self-contained. If we express this in terms of the anthroposophical understanding of child development seen as a process in which the child's soul and spirit nature gradually takes hold of and penetrates into its earthly physical body, then we can say that the child's 'incarnation process' may be supported and strengthened by such specially peaceful moments.

Just in this connection we can also be aware that the experience of giving and receiving spiritual healing is very much connected with *warmth* (see also the book *Spirit Healing* (Woodward 2004) in this respect), and it is the element of warmth which permeates our blood circulation and which, according to anthroposophy, provides the carrier or bearer of the human spirit – the ego. The ego lives in the warmth. So here again we see that this particular form of healing, *spiritual* healing, may very well stimulate or enhance the child's own warmth organism and thereby facilitate better ego-integration as an essential part of the process of incarnation. In the example of Peter we observed a very obvious and quite remarkable warming through of his normally cold hands and fingers in the healing sessions. He seemed to be very receptive and open to the healing energies.

To know, evidentially, the broader or longer-term effects or responses of any child with special needs to having regular spiritual healing sessions is, of course, not easy to assess because of all the other many factors which play into the child's totality of experiences and which can positively further his or her individual development and progress. In a Camphill Community setting the varied work and lessons in school, the soul warmth and life rhythms in the house-communities, the different specific therapies and medical treatments, and, very importantly, the sorts of interpersonal relationships which the child has with its carers and educators, all of these factors can contribute substantially to good progress seen over the course of a year. However, what can be seen and assessed, at least to an extent, is how a child is actually responding and behaving in the healing sessions themselves. I say to 'an extent' because not all that happens and transpires in a spiritual healing session will be outwardly visible or apparent. Certainly, unless the child with special needs is unusually articulate and able to tell us directly of his or her experiences, we can only make reasonable inferences from that which we can observe, feel and otherwise sense. The human being is after all wonderfully complex, is composed of many different parts and also embraces very different levels of awareness, from sleeping to waking consciousness.

As a healer and also as a curative educator, one tries to be aware of and to include the child's totality as a being of body, soul and spirit. Healing can indeed take place on all these various levels, some of which are deeply hidden to the outer gaze. Therefore a great sensitivity is called for in working with children with special needs, and due allowance needs to be made for subtle and gradual changes to occur over a period of time. In the case of many children who have multiple disabilities and particular medical syndromes, it is not a matter of effecting a cure or of somehow miraculously removing these deep-rooted conditions, but much rather of enabling the child's real being of soul and spirit to alleviate and overcome the limitations and restrictions which are imposed largely by the particular physical and organic constitution. An empathetic approach which acknowledges and understands the disabilities but which also recognises *the child's essential being*, is itself of the greatest curative value and both enables and empowers the child to 'move forward', and to gradually overcome certain obstacles and hindrances.

Spiritual healing recognises both the real spirit nature of the individual human being and also that real help can be called upon, and given, by spirit. The spiritual healer does not heal out of him or herself, but by becoming an effective and willing channel or instrument, for healing forces to be given to those in need of them. Healing forces which are directed and governed by spiritual intelligences, subject to certain laws and to the possibilities in the patient's particular circumstances of life. Just as the curative educator who works out of an anthroposophical understanding takes account of and can indeed call upon spiritual realities and beings to help, guide and strengthen him in his responsibilities and tasks, so likewise the spiritual healer can ask the spirit realm for the help which his patient specifically needs.

The healer acts then as the mediator, or link, to bring these good influences 'down to earth', so to speak, through the laying-on of hands in contact healing. To be permitted to give direct hands-on healing to children and young people with special needs requires particular sensitivity and tact on the part of the healer.

Some children and adolescents with special needs are very sensitive to being touched; even if they do not always show this same awareness when *they* take the initiative to touch others! The healer must therefore be ready to adapt or modify his or her approach and general procedure according to the needs of each child and the possibilities of the given circumstances, as has been shown in the descriptions of my own healing practice. There can be no question of imposition in this field of work but only of a willingness to give healing as far as the therapeutic situation allows and permits. Even when a child's parents or legal guardians have requested and consented to spiritual healing, this can still only be done if the child or youngster show themselves willing. As I already pointed out in the Introduction to this book, it is one thing to give spiritual healing to adults or youngsters who have freely asked for this and who are then able to give the healer informed verbal feedback as to any benefits they have received, and it is another thing to give healing to children and teenagers with special needs who are, mostly, not able to tell us of their experiences.

Instead of such personal feedback, very careful observations of how children are responding within the healing sessions, as well as additional reports and observations made by others who know the children well, are essential in order to sense how to proceed with the best interests of the child at heart. Clearly there are sensitive ethical issues in this therapeutic realm which of course not only have to be acknowledged in the application of spiritual healing, but in all areas of curative educational practice. In this respect I believe that my initial training and more than 30 years practice as a curative educator have been of immeasurable value in under-pinning and informing my more recent practice as a spiritual healer with children with special needs and learning difficulties. Children who not infrequently also show some challenging and testing behaviours!

I feel that I have been given a unique opportunity to offer spiritual healing to such children and young people. This has been possible through the openness of my colleagues to support such a new and unusual addition to our therapeutic and healing work within the Camphill School setting. However, I have tried to show clearly that spiritual healing is I believe in no way contrary or at odds with the holistic and curative educational phi-losophy of our school. It was indeed rather impressive to see how readily the parents of the children took up the opportunity to request healing sessions for their children when this additional resource was brought to their notice.

In concluding this chapter I will yet again make the important point that my own practice of spiritual healing has taken place within a broad therapeutic context which is specifically designed and shaped to provide the maximum benefit for the child who has special needs. Therefore cau-tion and reservation is needed when trying to assess any particular benefits for any particular child from spiritual healing *per se*. When some clear progress has been seen with an individual child, this progress I feel is largely due to the *combined efforts* of all those who work and live with children, including of course their parents and family, in such a way as to help bring about positive and healing changes. This is not, however, to say that it would be irrelevant to try to explore or investigate more rig-orously how any particular therapy, treatment or curative measure, including spiritual healing, may be contributing specifically to a child's further development and achievements. Indeed I think there is a real need for active research here in order to see better what is helping one particu-lar child and what, on the other hand, may not be helping this individual at this point in time.

What has been presented in this book does not as such, even with the very many examples of healing sessions, provide us with rigorous and systematic research into the possible effects and benefits of spiritual heal-ing with pupils with special needs. At the outset I made clear that the approach taken here was to be experiential, empirical and also anecdotal. This approach has nonetheless been based on some four years of practical experience in the field in which nearly a thousand healing sessions have been given so far.

This practical experience and my attempts to share something of it in this book can I think provide a very useful foundation for serious research and investigatory projects, such as I am myself currently engaged in. There is already contained in this book ample observational evidence that children and young people with special needs were helped to come to times of outer stillness and quiet in healing sessions and, though not proven, also by inference to a measure of inner peace.

As is apparent in the case studies, most of the children I have worked with were older rather than younger ones. That is to say they were already teenagers or adolescents. It would therefore be fascinating to see how young, or even very young pre-school children, might respond to spiritual healing interventions. Perhaps more could be achieved and greater benefits seen, if healing was given earlier in a child's development rather than left to later when a person can become rather more set and entrenched in their ways and constitution. This would certainly be something important to explore and research. Generally speaking, the earlier appropriate interventions or curative measures are started the better is the outcome for the child's individual development and progress. Perhaps healers, parents or researchers who read this book will be inspired to explore these possibilities – I hope so!

Conclusion

As I said in the Introduction, my purpose in writing this book was to share the experiences and observations gained in recent years in offering and giving spiritual healing to children with special needs, in the hope that this sharing might be of benefit to others – particularly of course to other children with special needs. I hoped also that the book would prove accessible and of interest to as wide an audience as possible, including fellow healers, educators, parents and professionals, who are concerned about and involved with the child or young person who has special needs and learning disabilities of one sort or another.

Although my healing practice has been set in a very particular environment and context, namely a Camphill School Community, I can very well imagine spiritual healing being offered and made available in a much wider and broader milieu. There are a large number of children who have some degree of special needs, and not all will have such severe and profound learning difficulties as some of those referred to in this book. There is a range of different provisions for these children, including of course some mainstream schools and colleges as well as more specialist places. The term 'special needs' includes a whole raft of aptitudes and disabilities including those which manifest on physical, emotional, behavioural and mental levels. There are, in short, many and diverse needs to be met.

The special character and quality of spiritual healing which sees a person holistically, and therefore takes account of the inner spiritual dimension as well as the obvious outer physical appearance, can have something of particular value to contribute and offer towards meeting such real and pressing needs. Fortunately we live now in a time when there is a widespread openness and interest towards a range of therapies and treatments such as homeopathy, acupuncture, reflexology and also healing, that can often helpfully complement more mainstream and orthodox approaches.

It is good once again to remind ourselves of the definition which is given in the *Code of Conduct* of the National Federation of Spiritual Healers: 'Spiritual healing is restoring the balance of body, mind, and spirit of the recipient. It is a natural, non-invasive, holistic approach that has the intention of promoting self-healing, to bring a sense of well-being and peace to the recipient' (2006, p.2).

I am not aware in the spiritual healing literature which I have come across so far, nor in the 'special' or 'curative educational' literature, of any application of spiritual healing in the field of special needs such as has been described in this book. Perhaps therefore what has been shared here may encourage healers, parents and professionals to consider spiritual healing as a resource that may be of service and benefit to some, if not all, special children. If it does so, and particularly if the results thereof prove fruitful, then this book will, I feel, have been well worth the effort it has taken to write it during these special Easter days. Whatever small effort this has entailed on my part, it is to the parents who have given me permission to refer to their son's or daughter's healing sessions with me and, above all, to the children themselves that I owe a considerable debt of gratitude. My thanks to you all especially.

Healing is not, I believe, a one-way process. The healer as well as the healee also receives healing help. Just as the curative educator knows that it is the pupils, the children or youngsters, who are actually his or her teachers, so similarly the healer has to thank his patients for the progress he is enabled to make as a willing channel for the Spirit – the Healing Spirit of unconditional Love.

In the final lecture, the twelfth, of the Curative Education Course of lectures given by Rudolf Steiner in 1924 in Dornach, we find the following words:

> Watch for yourselves and observe the difference – first, when you approach a child more or less indifferently, and then again when you approach him with real love. As soon as ever you approach him with love, and cease to believe that you can do more with technical dodges than you can with love, at once your educating becomes effective,

becomes a thing of power. And this is more than ever true when you are having to do with abnormal children. (Steiner 1998, p.214)

I believe that the impulse of love is indeed the common factor in genuine curative education and in genuine spiritual healing.

To be allowed to help create healing spaces – sacred spaces – where vulnerable children and young people with special needs and often restless behaviours, can find a measure of stillness, quietness and peace is, I think, without any doubt, a blessing and a grace.

Bibliography

Angelo, J. (2002) *Spiritual Healing – A Practical Guide to Hands-on Healing*. London: Godsfield Press.

Benor, D.J. (2002) *Spiritual Healing: Scientific Validation of a Healing Revolution – Professional Supplement*. Michigan: Vision Publications.

Bradford, M. (1994) *Hands-On Spiritual Healing*. Forres: Findhorn Press.

Buxton-King, A. (2004) *The NHS Healer*. London: Virgin Books.

Edwards, H. (1974) *A Guide to the Understanding and Pactice of Spiritual Healing*. Guildford: The Healer Publishing Company Ltd.

Hansmann, H. (1992) *Education for Special Needs: Principles and Practice in Camphill Schools*. Edinburgh: Floris Books.

Holtzapfel, W. (1995) *Children with a Difference*. Sussex: Lanthorn Press.

Jackson, R. (ed.) (2006) *Holistic Special Education: Camphill Principles and Practice*. Edinburgh: Floris Books.

König, K. (1969) *The First Three Years of the Child*. New York: Anthroposophic Press.

Luxford, M. (1994) *Children with Special Needs*. Edinburgh: Floris Books.

Luxford, M. and Luxford, J. (2003) *A Sense for Community*. Whitby, UK: Camphill Community.

NFSH (2006) *Code of Conduct*. Middlesex: National Federation of Spiritual Healers.

Pietzner, C. (ed.) (1990) *A Candle on the Hill – Images of Camphill Life*. Edinburgh: Floris Books.

Steiner, R. (1994) *How to Know Higher Worlds*. New York: Anthroposophic Press.

Steiner, R. (1998) *Education for Special Needs – The Curative Education Course*. London: Rudolf Steiner Press.

Strohschein, A. (1993) 'The Birth of Curative Education.' In *A Man Before Others – Rudolf Steiner Remembered*. London: Rudolf Steiner Press.

White, R. (2002) *Energy Healing for Beginners*. London: Piatkus.

Woodward, B. (2004) *Spirit Healing*. Edinburgh: Floris Books.

Woodward, B. and Hogenboom, M. (revised 2002) *Autism – A Holistic Approach*. Edinburgh: Floris Books.

About the Author

Bob Woodward was born in 1947 in Gloucester, England, and had his secondary education from the age of 11 at 'Wynstones', a Rudolf Steiner School in Gloucestershire.

In 1970 at the age of 23 he began as a student co-worker at the Sheiling School Camphill Community, in Thornbury, near Bristol. After two years he left there to attend the Steiner Teachers' Training at Emerson College in Sussex for one year, and then went to the USA to do the third year of the Camphill Training Course in Curative Education at 'Beaverrun', a Camphill School in Pennsylvania. After completing this successfully he returned in 1974 to the Sheiling School in Thornbury, near Bristol, and became the teacher of a new Class 1 with nine children with special needs, which he then took through to Class 8. Bob was a teacher for around 23 years and had several different classes. He has lived and worked in Camphill for some 34 years to date.

Whilst still teaching he undertook several courses of part-time study, first at Bristol Polytechnic where he obtained a Diploma in Further Professional Studies in Education – Special Education, and later at the University of Bristol where he was awarded a Master of Education degree and then, through research, a Master of Philosophy degree. Bob considers himself to be a perpetual student and learner and he is currently enrolled, part-time, at the University of the West of England on a research project to do with spiritual healing and children with special needs.

For the past 40 years he has also made a study of Rudolf Steiner's anthroposophy or 'Spiritual Science', having first read one of Steiner's fundamental books, *How to know Higher Worlds,* at the age of 18. Since 1973 he has been a member of the Anthroposophical Society in Great

Britain which is affiliated to the General Anthroposophical Society based at the Goetheanum in Dornach, Switzerland.

Since 2001 Bob has been a full healer member of the 'Bristol District Association of Healers' and he is also a healer member of the 'National Federation of Spiritual Healers' (NFSH), which was founded in 1954, and is acknowledged to be the principal organisation for spiritual healing in the UK, with more than 6000 members.

Bob is married to Silke and together they have five children who have grown up in Camphill, three of whom are now in their twenties and independent but still visit their Camphill home regularly.

He has many interests and his hobbies include: reading, writing, walking, jogging and collecting special stones and crystals. He has a particular interest in childhood autism and in 2000 he co-authored the book *Autism – A Holistic Approach* (Woodward and Hogenboom 2002).

Bob continues his practice of spiritual healing with children at the Sheiling School Camphill Community in Thornbury.